DON'T DIE
IN THE PEW

the Mystery of Israel and the
Deception of Eternal Security

"Wake up Sleeping Church"

KRISTA D. SMITH

Published by 2 Thrive Publishing Group
All rights reserved.
ISBN-13: 978-0692166833

Unless otherwise indicated, Scripture quotations are from the New King James Version.

Scripture taken from the New King James Version®. Copyright © 1982 by Thomas Nelson. Used by permission. All rights reserved.

Scripture quotations marked (NLT) are taken from the Holy Bible, New Living Translation, copyright ©1996, 2004, 2015 by Tyndale House Foundation. Used by permission of Tyndale House Publishers, Inc., Carol Stream, Illinois 60188. All rights reserved.

Scripture quotations taken from The Holy Bible, New International Version® NIV®
Copyright © 1973 1978 1984 2011 by Biblica, Inc. TM
Used by permission. All rights reserved worldwide.

Scripture quotations labeled KJV are from the King James Version of the Bible.

Scripture has been italicized to distinguish it from the authors thoughts. Brackets in Scripture indicate the authors descriptors. Scripture that contains bold font is intended to highlight the authors emphasis.

ACKNOWLEDGEMENTS

I am so grateful for the people that God has placed in my life for such a time as this. To my husband, Scott, I am thankful for your constant love and support. Teresa Gardner, our spiritual discussions have inspired me on a daily basis and have added so much to this effort. You are a bold woman of God, and I am blessed to call you my friend. Chris Grant, you are on fire for Jesus, and it is a wonderful site to behold. Thank you for continually sharing the truths you find in His Word. To all of the wise women of God that I meet for Bible study each week, thank you for being faithful to study the Word of the Lord with me. Your Christian fellowship and friendships are refreshing to my soul.

The prophet Isaiah assured King Asa, *"The Lord is with you while you are with Him. If you seek Him, He will be found by you; but **IF you forsake Him, He will forsake you**."*
{2 Chronicles 15:2}

CONTENTS

CHAPTER ONE

Why Write?

"Return to Me, and I will return to you" {Malachi 3:7 NIV}

When we hear the call of the Lord and respond with a humble and obedient heart, He will work in mighty ways. He'll do the things that only He can do. He will give wisdom, knowledge, and discernment to those who diligently seek Him. But, if we do not take time to grow and maintain a personal relationship with Jesus, we are truly deceiving ourselves. In essence, we are spiritually starving, and merely practicing "religion." If you've been walking with the Lord for any length of time, you know that the Christian life is a journey full of peaks and valleys.

My life has been a testament to the faithfulness of God. By the time I was just fifteen years old, I was on my own with no support from my family. I was married and divorced twice by the age of nineteen, and I had become a single mother. Through some very challenging times and humble beginnings, I learned to depend on my heavenly Father. As I was growing up and navigating my way in the world, the source of my confidence was thoroughly rooted in the promises of God. I believed what the Bible said with all my heart, and I would go to the Word of God for strength and wisdom. In the Scriptures, I read how the Lord would care for and bless those He loved and those who loved Him. I asked Him to help me often. And, He did.

My early experiences with Jesus forged a deep faith within my heart and soul. When I was reading my Bible, I wasn't just learning about religion or finding rules to follow, I was learning about my Savior. He was someone that I began to know in tangible ways, and to this day, I love and rely on Him. I find no greater joy than my time in His presence.

Fall has always been one of my favorite times of the year. I love watching the leaves change colors and layering clothes, but I especially look forward to the holidays around that time, including my birthday which is in September.

As my 30th birthday approached, my life had changed dramatically, and suffice it to say, I had a lot going on. It was 2004, and I was helping lead the youth program at my church, I had also recently started a local non-profit organization. I owned and managed a thriving mortgage company and a Christian preschool. On top of that, my husband and I were raising three young children. When my husband asked me what I wanted to do for my big day, I told him that I wanted to spend the day alone with the Lord. I had read about this experience in a book, and it sounded intimate and special. So, I thought that I would follow the author's example. Some of the ideas the book suggested were to take a walk, read the Bible, sit silently, and to write in your journal. The evening before my birthday, I was on the phone with my friend Traci Newkirk. She said, "The Lord told me what to give you for your birthday, so I'm going to swing by and drop it off."

She had prepared a basket with ground coffee, donut holes, prayer oil, and a devotional. I was thrilled by her surprise because I hadn't told Traci, or anyone else, how I planned to spend the day. Needless to say, her gift was perfect.

The next morning when I woke, I realized it was raining, so with a cup of coffee in hand, I grabbed my favorite blanket and made my way to a cozy place on the sofa. The house was silent. It was a perfectly peaceful morning. I opened my Bible to the book of Matthew and began. After reading through a few chapters, I was captivated. I couldn't stop reading. I had read the Bible often but I had never read full chapters at a time. I had listened to hundreds of sermons from countless pastors, but as I was reading on this particular afternoon, I could feel something was different. It was like a light had been turned on in my soul.

Later that evening my husband arrived home with the children, it was apparent that I had not moved from the sofa. In fact, I hadn't stopped reading all day. I shared my enthusiasm over what I was reading, and I ended up staying home from work for the next three days until I finished the entire New Testament. I was in awe.

While I read, I took copious notes to document everything the Lord was showing me. And, while the experience left me elated and infused, I also distinctly recall feeling deceived. For years, I'd trusted spiritual leaders for guidance, but as I continued reading, my eyes were opened to key parts of Scripture that had been left out of sermons. I perceived just how easily the Word of God could be misunderstood, twisted and taken out of context. Had I not gone to the Bible and searched the Scriptures for myself, without question, I would have continued to believe what I had been told, rather than what God's Word actually had to say. This was disturbing to me. So, I spent the next few days reviewing my notes and writing an outline of my findings, particularly the parts on salvation.

I was dismayed by my realization, but I wanted to seek wise counsel. So, I shared my notes with a few friends of mine who were pastors. I thought that since they had gone to seminary, perhaps they could tell me if I was missing something. And while I didn't get any feedback that contradicted my concerns, I also didn't know what I should do with the message. So, the outline sat on the hard drive of my computer for years.

The following week, I returned to my office, and coincidentally, one of the loan officers at my mortgage company was having an issue with a commercial loan for a local church. As I spoke with the pastor about the loan, our conversation shifted from business matters to spiritual ones. We had a three-hour meeting. At one point, Pastor Watson said, "I'm about to jump out of my chair. You're anointed. You're a teacher. I can feel it, and I can see it in you. You're a preacher." He was serious. I was truly shocked. First of all, me? Really? I prayed and told the Lord that if Pastor Watson's words were a message from Him, then I would need Him to confirm it. I didn't want to dismiss it, but I also didn't want to act on what had been said to me unless the Lord confirmed the message. I just wanted to know for sure that it was God. That evening I journaled, "Lord, I don't know where you're taking me, but I am willing to go... search my heart and purify me."

Ten months later, I had yet another unusual and unexpected experience. One of our clients left his I.D. in our copy machine. I saved it in my desk drawer, and I met him when he returned to pick it up. As we talked, he told me that he was a missionary and had recently returned to the U.S. Our conversation went on for two hours, and he eventually told me that God had given him the gift of prophesy. Before he left, we prayed. While praying, he said that he saw a vision of me with fire coming from my mouth standing in front of a multitude of people. He told me that in the vision, I was speaking the Word of God. He said that the message I'd written on salvation (the outline which he had never seen) was under the spirit of revelation. He said that I was a watchman and a warner to people in the last days. I journaled all of this, but I wasn't sure what any of it meant.

Three months later I experienced a vivid dream, and when I woke up, I could hardly contain myself. I immediately woke my husband to share it with him, and then I ran to my journal to write it all down. I had never experienced anything like this, and I knew it wasn't just an ordinary dream.

In the dream, I was standing outside in an open field with hundreds of people. It was early evening. Suddenly, lightning flashed, and we all looked up at the sky. I remember thinking that the flash might have been fireworks because it was so intense. Then, there was a tremendous burst of colorless light in the sky. It looked as if a distant planet had just exploded. Bursting from the light came hundreds of doves, and they descended towards us. The doves were adorned with the colors of a rainbow, and each bird was illuminated with a glowing light. The doves were small, like baby doves, and looked like they could fit in the palm of your hand.

I watched in awe and wonder as they quickly and gracefully descended. In my spirit, I felt like I was witnessing Jesus's return. I could feel the presence of God, and I desired to praise Him. I raised my hands to

13

worship, as did others. One of the doves landed in the palm of my hand, and I experienced a feeling of love that was so intense, I struggle to describe it with words. As I held the dove, my feet left the ground. I began to ascend into the sky, but I was the only person being taken which seemed odd. The people below me were saying, "Bye Krista." I felt a sense of relief that I was being rescued, but I also felt concern for the people left in the field. The next thing I remembered was the feeling of being carried. I was conscious, but my eyes were closed. I was being lowered back onto the ground, asleep. When I woke up, I was back in the same field, and all of the same people were lying on the ground sleeping.

As we all began to wake up (still in the dream), I felt filled with the Spirit. I remembered everything that had occurred, but no one else seemed to remember anything at all. Because everyone was acting as if nothing had happened, and since I wasn't exactly sure what was going on, I didn't say anything. Suddenly, people started to frantically organize themselves into lines. I saw guards approaching to make sure that we were all in compliance with something, but I wasn't sure what. So, I just got in line along with everyone else.

Then, I woke up.

I was sure that I had just experienced something spiritual. I prayed and asked the Lord to show me what the dream meant, and I asked him to help me understand what He was trying to tell me. I knew the Bible spoke of times when God revealed things in dreams and visions, and I also remembered how God had often provided an interpretation of these dreams. But, I was reluctant to share the dream, and so over time, I only shared it with a few people. I was hoping that the Lord might give some discernment of the dream to those I

14

shared it with. I told my friends Karina Samayoa and Clay Slatton. Karina was a close friend with a strong faith and an evident heart for God. Then, I told Clay, who was a friend that just happened to be a pastor. They both found the dream interesting and beautiful, but neither had any discernment as to its meaning.

I had another friend named Ken who was also a pastor that had moved to our area from Canada just a few years earlier. After I shared the dream with him, he said, "Krista, do you trust me?" I did, so I answered Yes. He explained that he had a dear friend in Canada who was a long-time spiritual mentor of his. He told me his friend was a Jewish rabbi who was in the process of relocating back to Israel to teach the Alpha Courses. Then he said, "He has the gift of interpreting dreams." Well, I have to say that I certainly did not expect that, but I had prayed and asked the Lord to give me understanding. Let me add that this still blows my mind, even today. What were the chances of this? I had never met anyone with the gift of interpreting dreams. I had also never met anyone who even knew anyone with this gift, outside of the Bible of course. Ken said, "I'm not going to tell him anything about you. I will just tell him you're a friend of mine and that you had a dream. He'll give you a call." I'll admit, I was open to the idea because the Bible says that interpretation of dreams is a real gift; however, I was proceeding with caution, nevertheless.

A few days later, I was at my office when I got the call. Ken's friend introduced himself and immediately explained that he was not always able to interpret every dream. He wanted to make sure I understood this, in case this turned out to be one of those times. He asked if we could pray first. As he prayed, he asked God to hold his tongue, but he prayed that when he spoke, that the Holy Spirit would only let him speak

15

that which was from the Lord. When I finished sharing the details of the dream, he told me that as I was speaking, the Lord had given him understanding. Without hesitation, he said, "The multitude of people in your dream represent those you will minister to at some point. The fact that the explosion of light was colorless represented the Word of God, which is pure and Holy. The rainbow-colored doves represented the presence of the Lord." He said a rainbow surrounds the throne room of God, and he told me that the rainbow also symbolized my destiny, just like Joseph's coat of many colors. He said that the fact that the doves were small represents something new God was going to do in my life. When the dove landed in my hand, it was symbolic of a new spiritual gift that the Lord was going to give me. Finally, he said, "When you ascended off the ground, this means the Lord will be the one to lift up your ministry, but it will be in His time. When you were lowered back onto the ground, the people that were asleep represented the Church." He said that the Church is asleep, and he told me that I have a message for the Church. When the guards came to check for compliance, this represented the spirit of legalism. He explained that my message for the Church would be met with much opposition.

As I reflected on the conversation, I sat in my chair, utterly amazed. The Church is asleep, and I have a message for it? I had fully expected this to be some sort of dream about judgment day, and I was at a bit of a loss about little ole' me having a message for the big ole' Church. I wasn't sure about that, and I didn't know exactly what it meant or even what I was supposed to do. But, I wholeheartedly believed that the Lord had a purpose and a plan for me, and I just needed faith. Until now, I've still not shared this dream with many people. I've generally kept it to myself because, frankly, Fed Ex did not just drop me off, and I realize that if you didn't know me, you might think I have a few screws loose. It took many years of compounding confirmation for me to be sure that the Lord was speaking to me. But, after everything that's happened, I think the only thing He has yet to do is to whack me in the head with a Bible and ask me if I'm listening.

I commissioned an artist friend of mine named Jared Emerson to draw the dream for me three years later. It had such an impact on me that I wanted to have a visual reminder of it. Over the course of the following decade, I experienced many seasons of life, and I'm certain that I was sifted along the way. In the years that followed, I've had all manner of ups and downs. I've experienced significant personal loss, and I've even had times of wandering. Through it all, I have always loved the Lord. But for a while, I got distracted by life and the cares of the world. I recently read a devotion which contained verses from Luke 22:31-32, and I was moved to tears. Jesus was speaking to Peter, and He said,

"Simon, Simon! Indeed, Satan has asked for you, that he may sift you as wheat. But I have prayed for you, that your faith should not fail; **and when you have returned to Me,** *strengthen your brethren."*

Peter (formerly known as Simon) failed for a moment, but in the end, his life would be counted a victory. The reasons for Peter's restoration and ultimate triumph rested on two things. First, Peter had a repentant heart, and secondly, Jesus had interceded in prayer for him. Jesus prayed that Peter's faith would not fail or be lost, but rather that it would remain and be strengthened. God is so good and so faithful even when we are not.

The Lord is concerned with building our character. Good character stems from the integrity of a pure heart, and it is always our character that determines the next steps that God will give us. Our disobedience is the only thing that prevents the next "something good" from coming to pass in our lives.

In late 2017, I had a wonderful weekend with a few of my best girlfriends at a "Women of the Word" conference in North Carolina near Lake Junaluska. As I sat on a deck overlooking the lake, I found myself speaking out loud to the Lord, confessing and repenting. I wept tears of remorse and then tears of joy. It was a turning point for me. I felt renewed and I was in total peace. The difference that I felt was in my own heart. I was no longer just remorseful. I had finally resolved to stop living life on my own terms. I truly wanted to live my life for Christ and make His purposes my priority.

Repentance is not feeling sorry for yourself, or even feeling sorry for those you've hurt. It's not even feeling sorry for the fact that you've broken God's laws by turning away from Him and serving only yourself. True repentance means being sorry enough to stop. As I continued to sit there in silence, in my spirit, I heard the Lord speak to me in a gentle but firm voice. He said, "You cannot serve both God and money." I've read this verse in Scripture before, but when I heard Him say it to me directly, it became more than just Scripture. It bothered me, and I began to ask God to help me understand exactly what He was saying to me. In other words, I was trying to understand what He wanted me "to do" in response to what He told me.

I've led a Bible study for years, but in my day job, I'm an entrepreneur. For two decades, I've been busy either building or running businesses. I wrestled with my thoughts, and I decided that I would be more intentional about spending time with the Lord. I also determined that I would take more time for others. The next session at the conference was led by Bible Teacher June Evans, and when she was finished, she closed out the evening with a time of prayer and worship. June was prophesying over some of the ladies in attendance. She placed her hand on me to pray and said, "The Lord wants you to walk in an area of 'not knowing.' He's going to ask you to do things you've never done. He is going to move you into doing something He has been preparing for you. He has plans for you like Abraham and Sarah. He has an anointing on you and is going to use you in mighty ways for the Kingdom." As soon as I was back in my room, I journaled everything June had said to me.

Seven months later, I was in the Smoky Mountains for a Women's retreat at the Cove. Our theme was "Awakenings." There were two questions that we were encouraged to ask the Lord. "What is God awakening you from?" and "What is He awakening you to?"

It was the last night of the retreat, and I was reading my Bible when I heard Him very clearly ask me a question in that familiar gentle, but firm tone. He said, "Who's Kingdom are you building?" The words pierced my heart. I knew what God was saying to me. It was only because of Him that I am where I am today, and this is something that I knew without any doubt. So, was He now asking me to give up the opportunities that He had given me? At that moment, the only thing I was sure of was the fact that I heard Him speak and that He was asking me to change my life's course. Even though I didn't know what my next steps would be, I had resolved that I would stop focusing on my own endeavors. I went home and resigned from my job in the mortgage industry.

Now, I'm certainly not saying or suggesting that the Lord expects everyone to quit their jobs. I believe He has different plans and purposes for each one of us. But, I am sure that this is what He asked me to do. I didn't have a plan, which is not usually how I operate. I always have a plan (just ask my husband). Without a plan, I just set off in the direction that I felt the Holy Spirit leading me. I decided to fill my days studying the Bible, reading books and worshipping the Lord. I had a wise friend tell me that they had never met anyone who had intentionally set out to spend more time with God and regretted it. I agree. There is nothing more fulfilling than the presence of the Lord and knowing in your heart that you are right where you are supposed to be, even if it's only for a moment. Soon after, I was on my sofa reading, and I felt compelled to revisit the outline I'd written in 2005. As I read through it, the Holy Spirit began infusing me with thoughts to fill in the gaps and expound on the message. This book is the result.

Throughout the Bible, it is evident that the Lord uses the weak things of this world to confound the mighty. {1 Cor 1:27} Scripture illustrates that He does not call the equipped, He equips the called. So, I have come to conclude that since He always used the most unsuspecting characters to deliver His message, and considering the fact that He even opened the mouth of a donkey to speak and accomplish His purpose, {Numbers 22:21-39} I trust that He can use me as well. I am confident in His ability, not mine.

In the book of Revelation, Christ was speaking to the seven churches and to each of them He repeated, *"He who has an ear, let him hear what the Spirit says to the churches."* The message given to each church was clear. The Lord is pleading with His people to "Repent." He continues to speak to the churches today. There is a tremendous difference between the practical reasoning that is based on the logic of this world and the counsel that comes directly from the Word of God. The Bible tells us that the Pharisees often spoke from their own thinking, rather than from God's Word. Because of this, Jesus told them they were leading people straight to hell. God keeps His Word and He has promised that He will accomplish every Word He has ever spoken.

Don't Die in the Pew!

CHAPTER TWO

Let's Reason Together

One of the things I love most about my pastor is that he always tells the congregation, "Don't take my word for it, go and see what the Scriptures say."

"Now the Berean Jews were of more noble character than those in Thessalonica, for they received the message with great eagerness and examined the Scriptures every day to see if what Paul said was true." {Acts 17:11 NIV}

There are two significant debates within the Christian faith today. Both of them affect our spiritual growth and our understanding of God's Word. These topics are often too uncomfortable for many church goers and too controversial for some church leaders. But, I do believe that in His Word, God speaks loudly and decisively on both matters. The first topic that this book will address is the "Once Saved, Always Saved" theology. This doctrine is certainly a point of contention and confusion. It goes something like this:

The moment a person genuinely 'accepts Jesus,' his salvation is secured. He faces no risk of ever losing his salvation, regardless of what he does, or doesn't do.

Once a person has been converted, all the sins he may commit in the future will not place his soul in any more danger. He may worship idols and commit murder, but because he has been "saved," he will still go to heaven. He will be with the Lord even if he never repents of those sins, and even if he continues in willful disobedience. However, let's say that a person does return to a lifestyle of willful sinning, it merely proves that this person did not have a genuine, saving faith to begin with.

Hmmm… Is this the truth?

This belief is being heavily promoted throughout the modern Church, but does the Bible actually support this doctrine of eternal security?

The second fundamental issue is Israel. There is an everlasting promise and a plan for Israel that has been orchestrated by God Himself. But, there are many Christians who believe that because of Israel's disobedience, the Church has replaced biblical Israel as the recipient of God's promises. This idea has been termed "replacement theology," and it teaches that the Church has replaced Israel with regard to God's plans, blessings and end-time prophecies. The problem with this theory is that it stems from human conjecture and supposition rather than the power of God and His unfailing Word. Less than 200 years ago, the idea of a restored Jewish nation was inconceivable. Today, and just as was prophesied nearly 2700 years ago, Israel is a thriving land. Its people have been re-gathered from all four corners of the earth. The native Hebrew language has been fully restored, as has Israel's original currency, the shekel. God specifically promised that each of these things would come to pass.

The land of Israel had been deemed a wasteland for nearly 2000 years, but today it is a flourishing oasis in the desert. Its ruined cities have been rebuilt. The fulfillment of God's prophecy around Israel is astounding. It is also indisputable proof of God's sovereignty, and it should encourage us to read and comprehend the Bible as literally as it was written.

I would like to take you on a biblical journey. While it may seem that the issues surrounding Israel and "Eternal Security" are unrelated, I believe that as you read this book, you will discover that they go hand in hand. We cannot fully understand what the New Testament Scriptures are telling us until we recognize the Lord's plan for Israel. Though the story of Israel begins in the Old Testament, it carries over into the New Testament. According to Scripture, salvation was made available to us only "because of" Israel. The Bible teaches that when we are counted as true believers, we become a part of Israel, just "as if we were natural-born children." It is important to know what we believe, and why we believe it. We need to be sure that our beliefs are rooted in biblical truth. The consequence of being wrong on this matter could be catastrophic and irreparable. Naturally, our human nature prefers the idea of eternal security, and of course, we would all prefer to be in the position of never being able to lose our salvation. However, taking any one biblical teaching and elevating it to the degree that it minimizes or overlooks other key doctrines, is a dangerous practice as it relates to our spiritual understanding.

If we are wise, we will personally analyze this position to determine if it aligns with what the Bible actually teaches. Is it possible that we, or even those we trust for spiritual guidance, might be interpreting and manipulating the Scripture to make it say what we want it to say? Could it be that we are defending and relying upon doctrine that well-respected men of the faith have, themselves, been taught in error? How often do we accept advice that seems reasonable and may even be appropriate but is actually contrary to the Word of God? A distortion is very close to the truth. A simple distortion can drastically and detrimentally alter the original intent. Many of us make time to read novels, self-help books, and educational manuals. But, we'll let the most important guide for our lives sit on a shelf where it is rarely, if ever, opened.

*"There is a way that **appears to be right**, but in the end it leads to death."* {Proverbs 14:12 NIV}

The assurance of our salvation is one of the most critical issues of our entire existence. If we have an interest and want to grow in our understanding and in our walk with Christ, we must train our Spirit with the truth of God's Word. When we function with the full Word of God, we operate in unity with Heaven. Let's be sure that our Christian experience is more than just a Sunday morning book club followed by brunch.

In one of her Bible studies, Christian evangelist and author Priscilla Shirer made a profound statement that has stuck with me. She said, "Our enemy disguises himself as an angel of light. He wants you to believe what he's telling you is God's will for you. He makes the lie so close to the truth that unless you have an authenticating light, unless you have an objective standard by which you run every thought, person, and decision under, you'll never be able to tell with your physical eyes what the truth is. The enemy disguises himself in the truth. Can you tell the difference between right and, almost right?"

Noted 19th century pastor Charles Spurgeon was referred to often as the "Prince of Preachers." He said, "Discernment is not knowing the difference between right and wrong. It is knowing the difference between right and almost right."

The Apostle Paul wrote nearly one-third of the New Testament. Scripture tells us that he often went to the people and to the churches to "reason" with them concerning the Scriptures. *"As was his custom, Paul went into the synagogue, and on three Sabbath days he **reasoned** with them from the Scriptures"* {Acts 17:2 NIV}

*"...Paul, having passed through the upper regions, came to Ephesus... And he went into the synagogue and spoke boldly for three months, **reasoning and persuading concerning the things of the kingdom of God**. But when some were hardened and did not believe, but spoke evil of the Way before the multitude, he departed from them and withdrew the disciples, **reasoning daily** in the school of Tyrannus."* {Acts 19:1,8,9}

The authors of the New Testament certainly do not condone being argumentative. However, arguing and reasoning are two distinctly different approaches. *"Don't have anything to do with foolish and stupid arguments, because you know they produce quarrels. And the Lord's servant must not be quarrelsome but must be kind to everyone, able to teach, not resentful."* {2 Tim 2:23-24 NIV}

Obviously, the discernment of the Word of God is not a "foolish or stupid argument." Regardless, we are instructed not to be quarrelsome about it. Instead, we are advised to be kind to everyone. We are advised to be kind and gentle in our delivery for the express intent of teaching people, correcting opponents and for gaining the knowledge of the truth. If you emphatically

27

believe that we are not saved by works but by grace through faith alone, I would like you to know that I agree with you. However, I don't believe we should stop there. Yes, it is a biblical reality that grace comes by faith alone, but this truth is simply the foundation. We must look deeper into the Word of God and pray for discernment. Otherwise, how do we apply the verses in the Bible that appear to contradict our foundational truth? For instance, what about the verses from the book of James?

"So you see, faith by itself isn't enough. Unless it produces good deeds, it is dead and useless...So you see, we are shown to be right with God by what we do, not by faith alone." {James 2:17;24 NLT}

If you are a student of the Bible, you may be thinking about Romans 8:38-39, which remind us that there is nothing in all of creation that can separate us from the love of God, and again, I would agree with you. Although, it is vital to recognize that everything described in this particular Scripture is an external force.

I wholeheartedly believe that no external force can separate us from the love of God. No-one. Nothing. Nothing can separate ME from God's love, except ME. I can remove myself from Him because I have free will. If our salvation is secured in spite of ourselves, then there is no such thing as free will. And, if losing our salvation is utterly impossible, then why do the very last words of the Bible say this? *"and if anyone takes away from the words of the book of this prophecy, **God shall take away his part from the Book of Life**, from the holy city, and from the things which are written in this book."* {Rev 22:19}

The mere mention of losing salvation is a source of intense debate within Christianity. As I've found out in writing this book, it is a source of intense debate among my friends. Undoubtedly, I strongly believe it should not be casually dismissed. The two views are on completely opposing spectrums. Essentially, it is a question of eternal security or false assurance. If it is true that once we are saved, there is no possibility to lose our salvation, then both types of believers are in good standing. On the other hand, if the position that one can lose his salvation is correct, then the heavenly eternity of many misguided or lukewarm Christians is in serious jeopardy. After all, it was Jesus who said the words, *"Not everyone who calls out to me, 'Lord! Lord!' will enter the Kingdom of Heaven. **Only those who actually do the will of my Father in heaven will enter.** On judgment day many will say to me, 'Lord! Lord! We prophesied in your name and cast out demons in your name and performed many miracles in your name.' But I will reply, 'I never knew you. **Get away from me, you who break God's laws.'"** {Matt 7:21-23 NLT}

Many things simply cannot be tied up into a neat theological box, but instead, they require spiritual discernment, wisdom and a thorough examination of Scripture. In a rebellious generation where the "Once Saved, Always Saved" theology is empowering many professing Christians to carelessly live a life that is identical to the principles of the world, answering the questions of eternal assurance may absolutely be our most necessary pursuit.

Throughout the Bible, we see a God who blesses obedience and curses disobedience. We see a God who pardons and a God who punishes. In this same vein, pastors are required to instruct with a balance of both assurance and perseverance. However, when people are given the confident assurance that they "absolutely cannot lose their salvation," mass numbers of professing Christians are being drawn into a complacent state of casual Christianity. The Word of God warns us that the Lord has no interest in our casual faith. He said that He prefers for us to be either hot or cold, but lukewarm is not acceptable. {Rev 3:16}

*"For a time is coming when people will no longer listen to sound and wholesome teaching. They will follow their own desires and will look for teachers who will tell them whatever their itching ears want to hear. **They will reject the truth** and chase after myths."* {2 Tim 4:3-4 NLT}

It can be a dangerous position to blindly follow the parade. We can look around our world and see that we are living in the smallest sliver of time that has ever existed. Jesus spoke about the coming deception and what the Church would look like in the last days. He tells us how people would only be interested in listening to what they want to hear. We know that He was speaking of religious people because He said they would "turn away from the truth" and that they would only listen to teachers who say what sounds pleasing to their ears.

Think about the world we live in today… how many churches offer motivational speaking and self-help type seminars rather than boldly proclaiming the truths in God's Word? Sure, they may use an uplifting Scripture or two to make their point, but what about the biblical call to put away our old lifestyles and live a transformed life? Have you heard people in the faith excuse their sin by rationalizing that God wants us to be happy? The truth is, God wants us to be in His Kingdom for eternity, and He will do whatever it takes to wake us up. Don't get lulled away from the Lord by pursuing a path that leads to your own pleasure.

Jesus said, *"You can enter God's Kingdom only through the narrow gate. The highway to hell is broad, and its gate is wide for the many who choose that way. But **the gateway to life is very narrow and the road is difficult, and only a few ever find it.**"* {Matt 7:13-14 NLT}

At this point, I believe it's important to clarify that this book is not necessarily intended reading for someone who does not already possess a relationship with Christ. If that's you, then I would suggest books that I've enjoyed such as "Experiencing God" by Henry Blackaby and "Believing God" by Beth Moore. I have written this book to help increase spiritual understanding for those who already realize God's great love for us. I mention this because you'll find a lot of theology and Scripture in the pages that follow, and the Bible has told us that it may be hard to understand for those who are untaught or unstable.

"...some things hard to understand, which untaught and unstable people twist to their own destruction, as they do also the rest of the Scriptures." {2 Pet 3:16}

The Bible says that some people are on milk and some are on meat. {1 Cor 3:2} In this verse, brand-new Christians are likened to infants. As a new believer, we begin by learning the simple, yet foundational truths of Scripture. Our spiritual eyes have just been opened. Because of this, we may not be ready for a college level curriculum. However, all are surely welcome to audit this class.

Jesus tells us how to become a Christian.

He says, *"If any of you wants to be my follower, you must give up your own way, take up your cross daily, and follow me."* {Luke 9:23 NLT} This is how we are to follow Christ. Christianity is not a gospel that is all

31

about us and what Jesus can give us or do for us, it's not about our self-fulfillment; it is quite the opposite. Denying one's self is not popular, and it doesn't market well, especially in today's "me-first" culture. This is the truth: We live by dying to ourselves. Jesus goes on to say that we need to take up our cross daily and follow Him. In this message, the cross is a symbol of death, and Jesus used it to illustrate the fact that we need to put our own desires to death, and instead, follow His plans and purposes. He said that whoever doesn't take up his own cross is not worthy of Him. {Matt 10:38-39}

Let's look back at Luke 9 verse 57. Someone says to Jesus, *"I'll follow you wherever you go."* Jesus replies in a way that ensures His followers know that they're not going anywhere fancy. He said, *"Foxes have holes, and birds of the air have nests, but the son of man doesn't have anywhere to lay His head."* He was saying, if you decide to follow me, you need to understand that it's not about you. In fact, Jesus was really saying that if we follow Him it may cost us everything. In the book of John's gospel, John memorialized a core teaching from Jesus. *"I tell you the truth, unless a kernel of wheat is planted in the soil and dies, it remains alone. But its death will produce many new kernels—a plentiful harvest of new lives."* {John 12:24 - NLT} The point Jesus was making is this, you have to die to yourself if you are going to be fruitful. He continued in verse 25, *"Those who love their life in this world will lose it. Those who care nothing for their life in this world will keep it for eternity."*

Everyone wants a Savior, but do you want a Lord? *"Come now, and let us reason together, says the Lord..."* {Isaiah 1:18}

As you prepare to journey through the pages in this book, I'd like to share that I'm not writing from a denominational perspective. I have filtered all that I have penned directly through the Word of God.

That said…Let's reason together.

CHAPTER THREE

The Mystery of Israel

We live in a generation that doesn't seem to have much patience for, or interest in, history. However, I would like to assure you that the history lesson in this chapter is worth your time and attention. Most Christians tend to ignore the Old Testament. Sure, most of us can recite the story of Adam and Eve or Abraham and Isaac, but does the Old Testament really apply today? After all, it's old and sometimes it gets a little violent. Often, it doesn't portray God as the benevolent, compassionate, and merciful God that the majority of Christians today prefer Him to be.

In this chapter, I will prove to you that we can't even begin to understand the New Testament if we don't first understand the Old Testament. Many of the verses used to teach from the New Testament are often misconstrued or misunderstood as they are explained to others. There is a common theme in this book, and it is this: The Bible must be read and considered in its entirety and in harmony with every other Scripture on any particular topic, lest the reader be in error. In short, we must be familiar with the Scriptures, all of them. And by the way, I didn't make that up, Jesus said, *"...Your mistake is that you don't know the Scriptures, and you don't know the power of God."* {Mark 12:24 NLT}

I would like to share with you the greatest love story of all time. As I studied it, I was in awe. After you read it, I believe you will be too. You may be thinking to yourself, what does this have to do with eternal salvation and the Christian debate over "Once Saved, Always Saved?" If we're going to understand the Word of God correctly, it must be rightly divided. And, if the Word can be rightly divided, then assuredly it can also be wrongly divided.

"Be diligent to present yourself approved to God, a worker who does not need to be ashamed, rightly dividing the word of truth." {2 Tim 2:15}

A primary component of rightly dividing the Word of God is to first establish who is being spoken to in any particular verse. There are three categories of people that are addressed in the Bible.

1) **The Jews**: God's Covenant People

2) **The Church**: Heirs of the Promise through Adoption which is comprised of both Jews and Gentiles who are no longer Jew or Gentile, but "one" in Christ.

3) **The Gentiles**: (a non-Jewish person) but also defined as heathens and unbelievers, unless and until they experienced conversion to Christianity.

All of the Bible is FOR the Church, but all of the Bible was not written to or about the Church. Yes, that's right, it's time to pay close attention. We need to build a proper foundation, so we can understand what the Scriptures are saying to us when we get into the New Testament. So, bear with me through the history part of this chapter, it is important. Don't read fast. Think about everything that is being said in the verses that follow. Trust me...you'll see.

The Kingdom of Israel was initially comprised of 12 Tribes and was ruled as one Kingdom under King Saul. Then came King David and, finally, David's son King Solomon. Each tribe was named after the sons and grandsons of Jacob. However, due to the fact that Israel continually disobeyed God's laws, the Hebrew people were split into two separate Kingdoms. In Jeremiah chapter 3, we learn that God calls Himself a husband to Israel, but it was also during this time in history that we discover God literally divorced her. *"Then I saw that for all the causes for which backsliding* **Israel had committed adultery, I had put her away and given her a certificate of divorce;** *yet her treacherous sister Judah did not fear but went and played the harlot also."* {Jer 3:8} So, her sister Judah was also a harlot, but she did not get divorced.

Let's bookshelf that information for the moment.

In 930 BC, the House of Israel became 'Northern Israel' and was comprised of 10 tribes. The tribes of Northern Israel continually broke God's laws, and they were eventually taken into captivity by the Syrians in 722 BC. They assimilated with the Gentile people of Assyria, and they dropped their Yahweh religion, as well as their Hebrew names and identities. As prophesy indicated, they lost their identity. The Bible also refers to Northern Israel as Ephraim. Its ten tribes included the Asherites, Reubenites, and Danites, along with seven other tribes. But, where are they today? They don't exist because they never came back from captivity, and for this reason, they are called the "ten lost tribes of Israel" even to this day. The Northern House of Israel did not understand the laws of God and did not keep them. Hosea 8:12 tells us that they considered the law a strange thing and could not understand it. This was because they had assimilated into the nations of the Gentiles, and therefore, they had essentially become Gentiles.

Israel's Southern Kingdom was represented by two of the twelve original tribes, Judah and Benjamin, and it was referred to as the House of Judah. The Bible tells us that one of the key differences in the House of Judah, was that the people of Judah understood and kept the law of God. {Gen 49:10}

In 605 BC, the House of Judah was taken into captivity in Babylon. And with that, the Hebrew kingdom which was established by God and had reigned in glory with King David had come to an end. Although, it did re-appear once more for a brief 70-year period in the second century BC, when the House of Judah resettled in Jerusalem. However, they were again forced into exile by the Roman Empire in 70 AD. Unlike the lost tribes, the people of the tribe of Judah did not lose their identity. Its tribes came back after their captivity, and they are the Jewish people of today. As prophecy foretold, they would be pushed into all four corners of the world. For centuries, it appeared that no Jewish nation would ever exist again. It also seemed that God had potentially broken the covenant promise He made with Abraham. Under that everlasting covenant, the Hebrew people were to share a special place in history, and they were to be the descendants of many nations. Homeless in the streets of Babylon, God's chosen people were in a time of confusion and despair. This period is memorialized as one of the most significant events in the history of the Jewish people: The Exile.

This time is aptly named. It was, indeed, the most extended exile in the history of humanity, and it continued into this past century. Prophecy tells us that in the end times, the Jewish people would once again be re-gathered in their homeland. The Lord promised to restore His people after He had scattered them throughout the earth. In 1948, nearly 2000 years later, and ever faithful to His Word, the Lord did return His people to their land. Thus, the modern nation-state of Israel was re-born. God is doing everything that He said He would do in the land of Israel right now, and without question, it is evident to an onlooking world that the ingathering is in full swing. {Deut 30:1-5}

"My God will cast them away because they did not obey Him; And they shall be wanderers among the nations." {Hosea 9:17}

So, back to our story. While the disobedience of the Northern Kingdom of Israel resulted in its entire disappearance, the two remaining tribes within the House of Judah retained their religion, practices, and their philosophies, even while in Babylon. They called themselves "gola," which means exiles, and they accepted the responsibility of their exile. They knew they had betrayed the Lord and had allowed the Mosaic laws and their practices to become corrupt.

As we continue, keep in mind that when we find Israel and Judah in Scripture, they are both of the original Kingdom of Israel. So, in later mentions, Israel refers to the Northern House of Israel and Judah to the South. In the books of Ezekiel and Isaiah, the prophets foretell that the Israelites would be gathered together again, and when that occurred, their society, religion, and the Davidic kingdom would be re-established. So, here's what I find surprising. Do you realize that everything that God has been doing from the Old Testament to the New is for and about Israel? God's promises were not initially given to the Gentiles. They were given only to Israel. God elected His people, He scattered them and then He predestined them to come back. {Is 45:4; 65:9; Acts 13:16-17} When Paul speaks to the Gentiles, he is talking to the scattered house of Northern Israel, those who had assimilated with the Gentiles and lost their Hebrew identities.

Jesus, Himself, identified who He was sent to save in Matthew 15:24 {NIV}, *"He answered, 'I was sent only to the lost sheep of Israel.'"*

Let's think about this for a moment. Jesus just said that He was "only" sent for Israel. So, what about John 3:16? For God so loved the world...the whole world. Who were the captives that were supposed to go out into the world? The 12 Tribes dropped the ball. So, the Lord sent 12 disciples instead. Interestingly, the only people we ever find referenced in Scripture as "sheep" are the Israelites. We can find that reference in Jeremiah 50:6 and Matthew 15:24.

So, with that in mind, let's read a verse in the New Testament from John 10:16, *"And other sheep I have which are not of this fold; them also I must bring, and they will hear My voice, and there will be one flock and one shepherd."*

Who do you suppose the "other" sheep are? I always thought this New Testament verse was referring to the Gentiles. It seemed like a fitting description. But, the sheep He refers to "which are not of this fold" are the tribes of the Northern House of Israel who had been estranged and divorced from God, and who, according to the laws governing adultery and divorce, could not come back.

When the Apostle James addressed his audience in James 1:1 he started by identifying who he was

40

speaking to. He said, *"To the twelve tribes which are scattered abroad."*

We established in Scripture that Yahweh, Himself, issued a certificate of divorce to Israel, but now there is a bit of a problem. In Jeremiah 3:1, listen to what the Lord says, *"They say, 'If a man divorces his wife, And, she goes from him and becomes another man's, may he return to her again?' Would not that land be greatly polluted? But you have played the harlot with many lovers; Yet return to Me," says the LORD."* He is speaking to Israel, and He is asking her to return to Him, but this is after He divorced her.

The problem lies in the law which the Lord had given concerning divorce. We find the law in the book of Deuteronomy. *"If a man marries a woman who becomes displeasing to him because he finds something indecent about her, and he writes her a certificate of divorce, gives it to her and sends her from his house, and if after she leaves his house she becomes the wife of another man, and her second husband dislikes her and writes her a certificate of divorce, gives it to her and sends her from his house, or if he dies, then her first husband, who divorced her, is not allowed to marry her again after she has been defiled. That would be detestable in the eyes of the LORD. Do not bring sin upon the land the LORD your God is giving you as an inheritance."* {Deut 24:1-4 NIV}

Houston, we have a problem! The law of God has been clearly stated, and yet in Jeremiah 3:1, the Lord has told Israel to return to Him, even after He has divorced her on the grounds of adultery. Surely, God would not violate His own laws. Yet, we find prophecies confirming that one day Israel will indeed return and be revived. But, how is this possible? God does not sin, and God does not lie. *"Return, Israel, to the LORD your God. Your sins have been your downfall! ...People will dwell again in his shade; they will flourish like the grain, they will blossom like the vine—Israel's fame will be like the wine of Lebanon."* {Hosea 14:1;7 NIV}

The entire book of Hosea is about the Northern House of Israel being scattered and then returning to the Lord. Let's go to the New Testament. As we read Scripture, remember that a Gentile is a non-Jewish person. *"You [Gentiles], by nature, were a branch cut from a wild olive tree. So if God was willing to do something contrary to nature by grafting you [Gentiles] into his cultivated tree, he will be far more eager to graft the original branches [Israel] back into the tree where they belong."* {Rom 11:24 NLT}

The Bible identifies who the olive tree is when the Lord is speaking of Israel. He said, *"I, the LORD, once called them a thriving olive tree, beautiful to see and full of good fruit. But now I have sent the fury of their enemies to burn them with fire, leaving them charred and broken."* {Jer 11:16 NLT}

*"For I will bring them from the north and from the distant corners of the earth...For I am Israel's father, and Ephraim is my oldest child...**Listen to this message from the LORD, you nations of the world**; proclaim it in distant coastlands: The LORD, who scattered his people, will gather them and watch over them as a shepherd does his flock."* {Jer 31:8-10 NLT}

We are about to read the New Covenant, but I want you to notice that the Lord did not say that He was making a covenant with the House of Gentiles. There is no House of Gentiles! But, hold on, God does make a way (by faith) for the Gentiles to be "grafted in" or adopted, if you will. I don't want to jump too far ahead, so let's bookmark that topic because we'll get there soon. *"Behold, the days are coming, says the LORD,*

*when I will make **a new covenant with the house of Israel and with the house of Judah**— not according to the covenant that I made with their fathers in the day that I took them by the hand to lead them out of the land of Egypt, **My covenant which they broke, though I was a husband to them,** says the LORD. But **this is the covenant that I will make with the house of Israel after those days,** says the LORD: **I will put My law in their minds, and write it on their hearts;** and I will be their God, and they shall be My people. No more shall every man teach his neighbor, and every man his brother, saying, 'Know the LORD,' for they all shall know Me, from the least of them to the greatest of them, says the LORD. **For I will forgive their iniquity, and their sin I will remember no more."*
{Jer 31:31-34}

We just read the covenant promise that God has given to us as believers, but it is important to note that it was originally given only to Israel. The indwelling of the Holy Spirit fulfills the promise. The following verse in Hosea is an Old Testament foreshadowing of the resurrection of Christ having the intentional purpose of restoring Israel. *"Come, let us return to the LORD. He has torn us to pieces but he will heal us; he has injured us but he will bind up our wounds. **After two days he will revive us; on the third day he will restore us,** that we may live in his presence. Let us acknowledge the LORD; let us press on to acknowledge him..."* {Hosea 6:1-3 NIV}

Prophecy foretold that, the lost tribes of Israel would be found among the Gentiles in the end-times. *"For surely, I will command, and will sift the house of Israel among all nations,"* {Amos 9:9}

*"Therefore, tell the exiles, 'This is what the Sovereign LORD says: **Although I have scattered you in the countries of the world,** I will be a sanctuary to you during your time in exile. **I, the Sovereign LORD, will gather you back from***

the nations where you have been scattered, and <u>I will give you the land of Israel once again</u>." {Ezekiel 11:16-17 NLT}

These prophecies are nearly 2700 years old! For 2000 years the Hebrew people were scattered throughout the Earth, and yet in our lifetime, God has fulfilled his promise and has re-established Israel as a nation in its ancestral land.

As Scripture foretold, the nation would be born in one day, and as history recorded on May 14th, 1948, it was. *"Who has ever seen anything as strange as this? Who ever heard of such a thing? **Has a nation ever been born in a single day?** Has a country ever come forth in a mere moment? But by the time Jerusalem's birth pains begin, her children will be born. **Would I ever bring this nation to the point of birth and then not deliver it?"** asks the Lord. "No! **I would never keep this nation from being born,** "says your God."* {Is 66:8-10 NLT}

Without examining all of the Scriptures, it is easy to misunderstand them. For instance, let's review 1 Peter 2:9: *"But you are a chosen generation, **a royal priesthood, a holy nation**, His own special people, that you may proclaim the praises of Him who called you out of darkness into His marvelous light..."* Guess who was being spoken to and about? It was not us, the Church. He was talking about Israel. And, this was not the first time a reference to Israel as a holy nation was recorded in Scripture. There is a term that will be familiar to biblical scholars, and it is the word "hermeneutical," which means the first reference of something. It is from the first mention that we are able, hermeneutically speaking, to identify an intended meaning. Let's look at the first mention of a "kingdom of priests and a holy nation" in the Bible. We find an identical description in the book of Exodus. *"And you shall be to Me **a kingdom*** *of priests and a holy nation.' These are the words which you shall speak to **the children of Israel.**"* {Exodus 19:6}

In the New Testament book of Romans, there is a similar reference. *"I will call them My people, **who were not My people**, and her beloved, who was not beloved. **And it shall come to pass in the place where it was said to them, 'You are not My people,' There they shall be called sons of the living God.**"* {Romans 9:25-26}

So, who was the Lord referring to when He says, "not my people?" In this New Testament verse, He was not referencing the Gentiles, nor the Church. He was speaking of the Northern House of Israel. We know this because He said the same thing to them in the Old Testament when the Lord declared, *"For you are not My people, And I will not be your God."* {Hosea 1:9}

He said this because He divorced Israel.

He continues, *"Yet the number of the children of Israel shall be as the sand of the sea, which cannot be measured or numbered. And it shall come to pass **in the place where it was said to them, 'You are not My people,' There it shall be said to them, 'You are sons of the living God.'"*** {Hosea 1:10}

Paul spoke of Israel's rejection of Jesus as the Messiah and he explained that it would not be final. He said, *"For I do not desire, brethren, that you should be ignorant of this mystery, **lest you should be wise in your own opinion,** that **blindness in part has happened to Israel until the fullness of the Gentiles has come in. And so, all Israel will be saved,** as it is written: "The Deliverer will come out of Zion, And He will turn away ungodliness from Jacob; **For this is My covenant with them, When I take away their sins.**"* {Romans 11:25-27}

Have you ever wondered why so many Jewish people throughout history have rejected Jesus as the Messiah? I mean, Jesus is Jewish, and aren't the Jewish people the ones He came to save?

We are given a clue in the verse we just read. Paul starts by mentioning a mystery, and he goes on to say, "that blindness in part has happened to Israel until the fullness of the Gentiles has come in." He is saying that the Jewish people will be spiritually blind during the time of the Gentiles [aka Church Age]. However, he is also saying that it will not be forever. It will only last until the time of the Gentiles is complete. I realize that it may not make sense to us, and we probably cannot comprehend why the Lord would cause Israel to be unable to recognize the truth, but He is God. He has a plan that is for their good and His glory, and we just have to trust Him, for He is trustworthy.

Let's go back to the divorce. God gave Northern Israel a certificate of divorce on the grounds of adultery He said she whored among the nations [served other gods]. Judah, on the other hand, did not get a divorce. In His anger towards the people of Israel, God decided to get rid of them and scatter them throughout the earth. But He said that at a later time, they would hear His voice and return to Him. This is a considerable problem. According to the Torah in Deuteronomy 24 [which contains God's law], once God divorced His bride, she can't come back because it would defile the land. This becomes one of the mysteries that Paul mentions. Despite the adultery and the divorce, the Lord tells Israel to return to Him. {Jer 3:1}

This is a dilemma because it appears that God is going against His own law. It remains a mystery until we get to Romans chapter 7. Paul starts his discourse in an unusual way, *"Or do you not know, brethren (for I speak to those who know the law)..."*

Paul begins this way to be certain that anyone listening would understand that in order to grasp what he is about to say, they must first know God's law. He knew that if they did not know the law, then they could not understand, they would misconstrue what he was about to tell them and miss the point entirely. He goes on, *"the law has dominion over a man as long as he lives? "For the woman who has a husband is bound by the law to her husband as long as he lives. **But if the husband dies**, she is released from the law of her husband. So then if, while her husband lives, she marries another man, she will be called an adulteress; **but if her husband dies, she is free from that law, so that she is no adulteress, though she has married another man.** Therefore, my brethren, you also have become dead to the law through the body of Christ, **that you may be married to another—to Him who was raised from the dead,** that we should bear fruit to God."* {Rom 7:1-6}

This verse is an excellent example of what Paul was talking about when he said that there are some things in Scripture that are hard to understand. We can easily misunderstand the significance of what is being said here. Some have actually interpreted this verse to mean that, as believers, we are now dead to the law entirely, and it no longer applies to us. In this particular Scripture, that isn't even close to what Paul was talking about. Remember, he very intentionally stated that he was directing this discussion to those who understood "the law." He clearly referred to a specific law, one that his audience of Jewish believers knew had caused the separation of the original 12 tribes of Israel. He specifically referenced the law of adultery which resulted in their literal divorce from God.

What is Paul saying? Dead to what law? He is telling his listeners that they are dead to the law of adultery, the law found in Deuteronomy chapter 24. He knew that the Jewish people listening, the ones who knew the law and the Scriptures, would understand what he was saying. Here, Paul is revealing the prophecy and the miracle of how the Lord was grafting them back in, as promised. He is saying to Israel, you were married, but you were unfaithful to your husband. You were an adulteress among the nations. Therefore, under the conditions of the law, you can't come back. But now, through the body of Christ and because of His death, you are freed from this law. So, you can now marry Christ who rose from the dead. What Paul has illustrated is the wedding for which we are all waiting. At this wedding, Christ will come for His bride, Israel and the Church, who will join Him at the marriage supper of the lamb.

Let's summarize:

- The Lord God was a husband to Israel {Is 54:5}.

- He divorced Israel for committing adultery, serving other God's and not keeping His laws. {Jer 3:1}

- According to Romans 7, the only way a woman can be freed from the law of adultery would be if her first husband dies. {Romans 7:2}

- The reason Jesus had to come as a sacrificial lamb was to die for His bride and to free her from the law because of her adultery.

- Remember, Jesus told us He was sent for "the lost sheep of Israel" in Matthew 15:24. When

Jesus rose from the dead on the third day, He became an eligible bachelor for the bride to marry.

Jesus dying for the lost sheep of Israel broke the curse of the law against the Northern House of Israel so they could be grafted back in, as prophesied. How beautiful and incredible is this!

So, where do the Gentiles (non-Jewish people) fit into God's Kingdom? The New Covenant is only with the House of Israel and the House of Judah. But, it is written, "...*For they are not all Israel who are of Israel,*" {Romans 9:6}. The Gentiles have been grafted in by grace through faith in Christ. Listen to this next verse in the New Testament as Paul is connecting the Gentiles to the New Covenant promise of Jeremiah 31. "*...for when Gentiles, who do not have the law, by nature do the things in the law, these, although not having the law, are a law to themselves, who show the work of the law written in their hearts...*" {Romans 2:14-15}

The Old Testament also prophesied about the Church, saying, "*It shall be that you will divide it by lot as an inheritance for yourselves, and **for the strangers** who dwell among you and who bear children among you. **They shall be to you as native-born among the children of Israel; they shall have an inheritance with you among the tribes of Israel.**" {Ez 47:22} The Gentiles are the 'strangers' referred to in Ezekiel 47, the strangers are grafted in and adopted as sons and daughters of the promise by their faith in Christ.

"*Yet to all who did receive him, to those who believed in his name, **he gave the right** to become children of God—*"{John 1:12}

We have been given "the right" to be children of God, but "the Gentiles" were never entitled. Therefore, we should not be haughty or arrogant about our secure position. One of the primary reasons for highlighting Israel's place in New Testament Scripture is so that we are correctly dividing the Word of God and not taking it out of context.

The Apostle Paul explains it best, *"But through their* [Israel's] *fall, to provoke them* [Israel] *to jealousy, salvation has come to the Gentiles...For if their* [Israel] *being cast away is the reconciling of the world, what will their* [Israel's] *acceptance be but life from the dead? ...You will say then, "Branches were broken off that I might be grafted in." Well said. Because of unbelief, they* [Israel] *were broken off, and you stand by faith.* **Do not be haughty, but fear. For if God did not spare the natural branches** [Israel]**, He may not spare you either.** *Therefore, consider the goodness and severity of God: on those* [Israel] *who fell, severity; but toward you, goodness, if you continue in His goodness.* <u>**Otherwise, you also will be cut off.**</u> *And they* [Israel] *also, if they do not continue in unbelief, will be grafted in, for God is able to graft them in again."* {Romans 11:11;15;19-23}

This verse tells us that if God would so harshly punish His chosen people, then we should not be over confident or haughty about our eternal security.

"For God does not show favoritism." {Rom 2:11}

Paul says that God will continue in goodness towards us under one condition. That is, "if" we also continue in goodness. Otherwise, we're at risk to suffer the same consequence as the Israelites, and we will be cut off from God. Paul is poignantly explaining that if God did not spare the people that He most cherished, what would make us think that He will spare us, IF we choose to live life on our own terms and IF we do not remain in Him.

The promises of the covenant are available to us if we come by faith in Christ. The bottom line is that once we have been grafted into God's family, then we are all one in Christ. The Gentiles will share in the inheritance promised to the tribes of Israel, just as if they were native-born. Through our adoption, we become part of God's Holy nation, ISRAEL! *"There is neither Jew or Gentile, neither slave or free, nor is there male and female, for you are all one in Christ Jesus."* {Gal 3:28 NIV}

"Let us rejoice and be glad and give the glory to Him, for the marriage of the Lamb has come and His bride has made herself ready." It was given to her to clothe herself in fine linen, bright and clean; **for the fine linen is the righteous acts of the saints.** *Then he said to me, "Write,* **'Blessed are those who are invited to the marriage supper of the Lamb** *'" And he said to me,* **"These are true words of God."** {Rev 19:7-9}

We have established in both Testaments that the covenants and promises were initially established with the House of Israel and the House of Judah. When we come to Christ by faith, we become a sheep in His fold. Christ becomes our good Shepard, and have become children of the promise. But, throughout Scripture, we are strongly advised that we must remain in Christ. We should also understand that time on this earth is measured by what God is doing with Israel. *"For behold, the days are coming,' says the Lord, 'that I will bring back from captivity My people Israel and Judah,' says the Lord. 'And I will cause them to return to the land that I gave to their fathers, and they shall possess it... And I will punish all who oppress them.'"* {Jer 30:3,20}

The Lord did not just prophesy over the people. He even prophesied to the land itself. I didn't know that mountains could hear, but I guess they can.

*"But **you, mountains of Israel**, will produce branches and fruit for my people Israel, for they will soon come home. I am concerned for you and will look on you with favor; you will be plowed and sown, and I will cause many people to live on you—yes, all of Israel. The towns will be inhabited and the ruins rebuilt. I will increase the number of people and animals living on you, and they will be fruitful and become numerous. **I will settle people on you as in the past and will make you prosper more than before.** Then you will know that I am the LORD... Therefore say to the Israelites, 'This is what the Sovereign LORD says: **It is not for your sake, people of Israel, that I am going to do these things, but for the sake of my holy name,** which you have profaned among the nations where you have gone...The desolate land will be cultivated instead of lying desolate in the sight of all who pass through it. They will say, 'This land that was laid waste has become like the garden of Eden; the cities that were lying in ruins, desolate and destroyed, are now fortified and inhabited.' **Then the nations around you that remain will know that I the LORD have rebuilt what was destroyed and have replanted what was desolate. I the LORD have spoken, and I will do it."***
{Ez 36:8-11,22,34-36 NIV}

The Lord is doing this right now, in this generation, and right before our eyes. The people of Israel have been returned to their homeland, and we have seen Israel's ruined cities rebuilt. The Lord has restored the original Hebrew currency and Hebrew language, just as prophesied. This language had not been spoken since the 2nd Century until it was restored in the 19th Century. It was revived by Eliezer Ben Yehuda in 1881.

*"Thus says the Lord of hosts, the God of Israel: "**They shall again use this speech in the land of Judah** and in its cities, **when I bring back their captivity**: 'The Lord bless you, O home of justice, and mountain of holiness!'"* {Jer 31:23}

All of these promises have been sitting within the pages of Scripture for more than 2000 years. The prophecy regarding the exiled Israelites returning to their land had been unfulfilled, until now. Israel was a deserted wasteland of desolation and ruins from the era of Jesus' day until it became a nation on May 14, 1948. We are witness to a modern-day miracle, and it should stir us to learn what God has in store for Israel because it will directly affect us, the Church. Christianity cannot explain its roots without Judaism. We have Jewish roots. It is not possible to say, "I am a Christian" in sincerity and truth, yet simultaneously have no love or care for the plight of the Jewish people. There is no such thing as Christian anti-Semitism because it is only hatred and ignorance of God's Word that drives anti-Semitism.

I had the privilege to attend the Washington Summit for the celebration of Israel's 70th anniversary. During the conference, we learned that even within the Church, there has been a willful lack of teaching about Israel and God's plans for the future. One of the well-known speakers shared that most seminaries and Bible colleges don't teach ministers on the subject of how modern-day Israel fits into biblical prophecy. This may be a result of the "replacement theology" which has pervaded Christianity since the time of Martin Luther. This replacement theology was founded on the belief that the Church has permanently replaced Israel relative to the plan, purposes, and promises of God. This position is entirely heretical. The Lord has not removed Israel or replaced her. He IS doing exactly what He said that He would do as it relates to Israel. The Lord said that He would scatter His people due to their disobedience, and as a result, they would suffer His wrath. But, He promised that at a later time, He would show them mercy. He would re-gather them from all corners of the earth and He would assemble them as a nation in their ancestral land. *"This is what the LORD Almighty says: 'Just as I had determined to bring disaster on you and showed no pity when your ancestors angered me,' says the LORD Almighty, 'so now I have determined to do good again to Jerusalem and Judah [Israel]. Do not be afraid.'"* {Zech 8:14-15 NIV}

He chose Israel and set her apart. He did this to show Himself as God to the world. He stayed true to His Word to demonstrate His power and faithfulness. It is time for us to wake up. The Lord is showing us that He keeps His promises. We are wise if we pray and ask the Lord to open our eyes and to show us the truth. Mark Twain wisely said, "If you don't read a newspaper or watch the news you will be uninformed, and if you do read a newspaper or watch the news you will be misinformed." The only place we can find the timeless truth is in the Word of God.

"For the gifts and the calling of God are irrevocable." {Romans 11:29}

If you read verses 11:25-32 in Romans, you will find that it is Israel who is being referenced in this Scripture. Israel's place in God's promise is irrevocable. *"I will bless those who bless you [Israel], And I will curse him who curses you; And in you [Israel] all the families of the earth shall be blessed."* {Gen 12:3}

Do you realize all the blessings that have come to the world from this young, and tiny Nation of Israel which is only about the size of New Jersey and is just

54

70 years old? The medical and technological advancements coming out of Israel are unbelievable.

The people of Israel have created the USB flash drives, antivirus software, the artificial cornea, instant messaging technology, the first bone implant, robotic exoskeleton for paraplegics, a navigation smartphone app, the pill-cam, the first Voice over IP internet phone software, iron dome mobile air defense system, solar water heater, drip irrigation methods, electronic milk meter for dairy farmers...and the list could go on and on. Israel has produced 12 Nobel Prize winners since 1966. Israel is 3rd behind the US and China with the most companies listed on the Nasdaq. Israel is truly a miracle blossoming in the desert of the Middle East, and from it, the families of the earth are being blessed.

"Indeed, He who watches over Israel never slumbers or sleeps." {Psalm 121:4 NLT}

The question that many of us have is why? Why would Israel be raised? Why would Israel be blessed when it turned its back on God? Well, the answer is pretty simple: It's because God said so. He is faithful to keep His promises. He made an everlasting covenant [for a thousand generations] with Abraham and that covenant had nothing to do with Israel's faithfulness. *"Know therefore that the Lord your God is God; he is the faithful God, keeping his covenant of love to a thousand generations of those who love him and keep his commandments. But those who hate him he will repay to their face by destruction; he will not be slow to repay to their face those who hate him. **Therefore, take care to follow the commands, decrees and laws I give you today.**"* {Deut 7:9-11 NIV}

He is blessing Israel for His own name's sake. He is keeping His Word and has chosen Israel to reveal

His faithfulness to all of creation. *"And the nations will know that the people of Israel went into exile for their sin, because they were unfaithful to me. So I hid my face from them and handed them over to their enemies, and they all fell by the sword. I dealt with them according to their uncleanness and their offenses, and I hid my face from them. "Therefore this is what the Sovereign Lord says: I will now restore the fortunes of Jacob [Israel] and will have compassion on all the people of Israel, and I will be zealous for my holy name. They will forget their shame and all the unfaithfulness they showed toward me when they lived in safety in their land with no one to make them afraid. When I have brought them back from the nations and have gathered them from the countries of their enemies, I will be proved holy through them in the sight of many nations. Then they will know that I am the Lord their God, for though I sent them into exile among the nations, I will gather them to their own land, not leaving any behind. I will no longer hide my face from them, for I will pour out my Spirit on the people of Israel, declares the Sovereign Lord."* {Ez 39:23-29 NIV}

We should also consider the significance of the time in which we are living. *"They [Israel] will be killed by the sword or sent away as captives to all the nations of the world. And Jerusalem will be trampled down by the Gentiles until the period of the Gentiles comes to an end."* {Luke 21:24 NLT}

Yep, you read that right. So, what does it mean? The "period of the Gentiles" coming to an end is a reference to the end-times. The fact that the Jewish people have been re-gathered in their ancestral land exactly as God promised over 2000 years ago is a significant place on the prophetic timeline. It is also a good indication that the period of the Gentiles is at the finish line.

It is time for the Church to Wake Up!

The disciples asked Jesus about the end of the Age. They asked Him how we could know when "the time of the end" was about to take place. Jesus tells them a parable of the fig tree. The fig tree is the country symbol for Israel, just like the Eagle is the symbol for the US, and the Bear is the symbol for Russia.

"Teacher," they asked, "when will all this happen? What sign will show us that these things are about to take place? ...Jesus answered, He spoke to them a parable: **"Look at the fig tree** *[Israel], and all the trees* [other Nations spoke of by Old Testament Prophets]. **When they are already budding** [when we see Israel become a nation and other nations lining up in their prophetic places], *you see and know for yourselves that* **summer** *[return] is now near. So, you also, when you see these things happening, know that* **the kingdom of God is near.** *Assuredly, I say to you, this generation* [a lifespan of people is no more than 100 years] **will by no means pass away till all things take place.** *Heaven and earth will pass away, but My words will by no means pass away."* {Luke 21:7,29-33}

• The generation that witnessed Israel become a nation in 1948 and has seen her budding in her own land as prophesied, is still alive today. Scripture tells us that this generation will not pass away, meaning that when Jesus returns, there will still be people living that saw Israel become a nation. If you're thinking, *"no man knows the day or the or the hour"*, that is correct. But Jesus said many times, "when you see these things happen," know that I am at the door. He warned us to be watching for His return. He also said we are wise if we are found doing what He has called us to do when He comes. His promises are real. He keeps them. He is at the door.

57

There is one final point I'd like to make as we bring this chapter to a close. Is it possible that we can become so familiar with Scripture that we may misunderstand it, even unintentionally? This can profoundly affect our spiritual growth. There is a verse that is used in conversations, cards, and even in email signatures. It has been framed and hangs on the walls in countless homes. Coincidentally, it has been my life verse.

"For I know the thoughts that I think toward you, says the LORD, thoughts of peace and not of evil, to give you a future and a hope." {Jer 29:11}

I love this verse. It is for me because I am a child of the promise through Christ. But, in order to discover who the Lord was originally speaking to, we need to start back at verse 4. *"Thus says the LORD of hosts, the God of Israel, **to all who were carried away captive, whom I have caused to be carried away from Jerusalem to Babylon:** ... For thus says the LORD: After seventy years are completed at Babylon, I will visit you and perform My good word toward you and cause you to return to this place. **For I know the thoughts that I think toward you, says the LORD, thoughts of peace and not of evil, to give you a future and a hope.** Then you will call upon Me and go and pray to Me, and I will listen to you. And you will seek Me and find Me when you search for Me with all your heart. I will be found by you, says the LORD, **and I will bring you back from your captivity; I will gather you from all the nations and from all the places where I have driven you, says the LORD, and I will bring you to the place from which I cause you to be carried away captive."* {Jer 29:4,10-11}

Let's not forget that God still loves, keeps and cares for Israel. It is because of Israel's fall that we have been given "the right" of adoption into the Kingdom. As the Church, we now have parallel promises, but in order to understand what the Bible is telling us, we need to acknowledge who had them first.

Father open our eyes to see and our ears to hear. Give us wisdom, understanding, and knowledge in the deep truths within Your Word and Your revelations. In the mighty name above every other name. Amen!

CHAPTER FOUR

The Road Map

In the last chapter, we strolled down the ancient paths to better understand Israel and how God's plan for them is written throughout the Old and the New Testaments. Foundationally, we have also established the importance of rightly dividing the Word of God by:

1) confirming context, and

2) by discovering who it is that is being spoken to or about.

Within this chapter, I've summarized the theology you'll find throughout this book. Maps can be a helpful resource to guide us in our understanding and to help us find our way. I intend to use the Word of God to illuminate our path. As we continue our study, we'll consider some significant truths. I believe it is more important to hear what the Lord has to say, rather than what Krista has to say. So, throughout this expedition, you'll find a lot of Scripture embedded along the trail. I'm merely the guide being used to put it in order.

For the intended purpose of staying on track and keeping to the point, this book does not dwell on the love that God has towards us. However, first and foremost, we must build every facet of our faith on the foundation of His steadfast and unwavering love for us. It is stronger than death. He chose us before we chose Him, and His love for us does not depend on our response to Him. With that core principle established, let's get started.

"If you declare with your mouth, "Jesus is Lord," and believe in your heart that God raised him from the dead, you will be saved." {Rom 10:9 NIV}

<u>Step Number 1 is Faith:</u> The requirement for salvation is repentance through faith in Jesus Christ as Lord. We receive forgiveness solely because of His grace towards us. *"For it is by grace you have been saved, through faith — and this is not from yourselves, it is the gift of God — not by works, so that no one can boast."* {Eph 2:8-9 NIV}

No human efforts can pay the price to obtain the gift of eternal life. There is nothing any of us can do, no matter how kind or generous we are. This gift is freely given to anyone who calls upon the name of the Lord Jesus in repentance. It's yours! It's mine! It's true. No one can take it from us! It is not possible for anyone or anything to separate us from the love of Christ. The Holy Spirit remains with us, regardless of the choices we make. We will feel the spirit convicting us when we do something sinful. We can, however, quiet His voice by squelching the Spirit and by continually ignoring the convictions which are intended to lead us to repentance. We can freely choose our path in life, and the Lord will not forsake us. He will wait for us and gently draw us back, if we are willing to return.

<u>Step Number 2 is Lordship:</u> If we abide in Him, and He abides in us, we will be doers of His word. If our faith is sincere, it will naturally lead to obedience. This obedience is not out of obligation; it is out of our love relationship with Him. If we truly love someone, we will naturally desire to please them. However, if our love goes no further than our lips, it is a delusion and will not save our soul. Many reject the truths of the Bible, and at the same time, they profess great love for Jesus. *"These people draw near to Me with their mouth, and honor Me with their lips, but their heart is far from Me. And in vain they worship Me, Teaching as doctrines the commandments of men."* {Matt 15:8-9}

*"And we can be sure that we know him **if** we obey his commandments. If someone claims, "I know God," but doesn't obey God's commandments, that person is a liar and is not living in the truth. **But those who obey God's word truly show how completely they love him. <u>That is how we know we are living in him.</u>** Those who say they live in God should live their lives as Jesus did."* {1 John 2:3-6 NLT}

In the verse above, notice there is both a promise and a condition, and also note that they are separated by the word "if." This is a great example of an obvious condition of God's promise. Many of us talk to our own children in the same way. We say, "You will get your allowance, IF, you do your chores." "I will continue to pay for your college, IF, you maintain a good GPA." But, if our children don't do their chores, then guess what? There is no allowance. As human parents, we understand the importance of boundaries, discipline and consequences. Spiritually, the concept is no different.

Simply stated, we can no longer continue to live a sinful lifestyle. Once we have learned the truth of the Word, we are held to a higher standard. *"But someone who does not know, and then does something wrong, will be punished only lightly. When someone has been given much, much will be required in return; and when someone has been entrusted with much, even more, will be required."* {Luke 12:48 - NLT}

We are equipped and enabled to overcome sin altogether. Throughout the Bible, the Lord has clearly revealed "His will." We have been given a guide, the Bible. If we read it, we should not be confused about the right thing to do. He has placed the Holy Spirit in us to lead us in our decisions and to convict us when we are not in line with God's Word. It is by His Spirit dwelling in us that we become capable of withstanding the devil and his temptations. The Bible tells us to put on the whole armor of God. This is not merely a poetic statement. The weapons of our warfare are not physical weapons. We can be equipped with real spiritual armor to withstand real spiritual battles. We start by girding ourselves with the truth found in the Word of God. *"Stand firm then, with the belt of truth buckled around your waist, with the breastplate of righteousness in place"* {Eph 6:14}

His grace is enough and sufficient in the fullest sense. We may continue to sin, but if we are in close fellowship with Him and He has Lordship over our lives, we will immediately feel the conviction of our wrongs by His Spirit. When we respond to the awareness of our sin by repenting, the slate is made clean again. This cleansing is all due to the work of Christ on the cross. Keep in mind that repentance is an attitude of the heart, and the Lord searches the heart. *"For the kind of sorrow God wants us to experience leads us away from sin and results in salvation. There's no regret for that kind of sorrow.* **But worldly sorrow, which lacks repentance, results in spiritual death.**" {2 Cor 7:10}

"Therefore, to him who knows to do good and does not do it, to him it is sin." {James 4:17}

To repent means to turn around altogether and to go the opposite way. When we recognize our sin, the Bible does not speak of re-dedicating ourselves, it says to Repent! ***"Those whom I love I rebuke and discipline. So be earnest and repent."*** {Rev 3:19 NIV}

True repentance is not a wishful resolution; it is a decisive change in one's course. If we continue to willfully sin, we have not experienced true repentance. The evidence of the condition and attitude of our heart is an active response to God's Word. We are agreeing with what the Bible says about our sin, and we are making a conscious effort to align ourselves with His will for us. *"For we have become partakers of Christ if we hold the beginning of our confidence* **steadfast to the end,** *while it is said: "Today if you will hear His voice, do not harden your hearts as in the rebellion."* {Hebrew 3:14-15}

"We then, as workers together with Him also **plead with you not to receive the grace of God in vain.**" {2 Cor 6:1}

The gift of Salvation is given by the grace of God. This gift should not be received light-heartedly. The definition of the word "vain" is something that produces no result, something that is useless. "Saving faith" is permeated with repentance. If we are abiding in Jesus as the Lord of our lives, we will be repentant when we've sinned because we will be sensitive to the promptings of the Spirit. Some may challenge this truth by arguing that if we must be obedient, AND we are expected to produce works in order to earn salvation, then the gift of salvation is not actually free. On the contrary, it is indeed a free gift. Forgiveness comes from a humble and repentant heart bowing down to Jesus for the remission of sins. Nothing else is required on our part. He knows if our heart is truly repentant. But, it is vital to remember that in order "to remain" in fellowship with Christ, *we must become doers of the word and not hearers only, deceiving ourselves."* {James 1:22}

Paul said, *"So I tell you this, and insist on it in the Lord, that **you must no longer live as the Gentiles do**, in the futility of their thinking. They are darkened in their understanding and **separated from the life of God because of the ignorance that is in them** due to the hardening of their hearts. Having lost all sensitivity, they have given themselves over to sensuality so as to indulge in every kind of impurity, and they are full of greed. That, however, is not the way of life you learned when you heard about Christ and were taught in him in accordance with the truth that is in Jesus. **You were taught, with regard to your former way of life, to put off your old self, which is being corrupted by its deceitful desires; to be made new in the attitude of your minds; and to put on the new self, created to be like God in true righteousness and holiness.** Therefore, each of you must put off falsehood and speak truthfully to your neighbor, for we are all members of one body. "In your anger do not sin"': Do not let the sun go down while you are still angry, and do not give the devil a foothold. Anyone who has been stealing must steal no longer, but must work, doing something useful with their own hands, that they may have something to share with those in need. Do not let any unwholesome talk come out of your mouths, but only what is helpful for building others up according to their needs, that it may benefit those who listen. And do not grieve the Holy Spirit of God, with whom you were sealed for the day of redemption. Get rid of all bitterness, rage, and anger, brawling and slander, along with every form of malice. Be kind and compassionate to one another, forgiving each other, just as in Christ God forgave you."* {Eph 4:17-32 NIV}

We are given guidance in Scripture. And, yes, I realize that we just read a verse that says we are "sealed for the day of redemption." We will explore this verse in a later chapter. However, keep in mind that it says you are "sealed for" the day of redemption. On that day, you will need to be redeemed, but until then, you are not yet redeemed. Basically, you have a reservation in heaven. For example, I can make a down payment on a vehicle, and the dealership will hold the car for me. However, when I arrive at the dealership, I'll be asked to produce the means to pay the balance.

Similarly, if I have "remained in Christ" then He will redeem me, and my debt will be covered in full. When we die and stand before the Lord, the writings or teachings of any well-known author, parent, pastor or evangelical leader will be irrelevant. The only thing that is going to stand is the Word of God and how we personally responded to what the Lord taught us in His Word. We've got to wake up and open our Bibles. *"Brethren, if anyone among you **wanders from the truth**, and someone turns him back, let him know that he who turns a sinner from the error of his way will **save a soul from death** and cover a multitude of sins."* {James 5:19-20}

If falling from grace were impossible, it would make little sense for James to have made this point at all. When he uses the words "anyone among you…", He is speaking to the believers, his fellow sojourners within the faith. One cannot be a "wanderer from the truth" if he never had the truth in the first place. He says, "and someone turns him back, let him know that the person who turned him back **saved a soul** from death." In this portion of the verse, James is clearly not speaking to unbelievers. He is explaining the serious consequences for those who already "have" the truth and then wander from it. To avoid death, they must go "back" to where they were.

Death in the Greek is, Thanatos (than'-at-os) meaning: death, physical or spiritual.

In every generation, many people have believed that in order to obtain salvation, they must earn favor with God through their good works. Even today, this belief persists in many denominations. However, in the Bible we learn that grace by faith plus works is a false teaching! But also, the Bible says that faith without works is dead. So, just what does the Bible say exactly, and which statement is correct?

"For by grace you have been saved through faith, and that not of yourselves; it is the gift of God, not of works, lest anyone should boast." {Eph 2:9}

"Thus also faith by itself, if it does not have works, is dead… But do you want to know, O foolish man, that faith without works is dead?" {James 2:17; 20}

First of all, in order to understand this, we must first understand the biblical definitions of "justification" and "sanctification." Secondly, we need to realize that they each have entirely different meanings and purposes altogether. It is when we receive grace by faith that we are justified by an unmerited favor, and immediately pronounced righteous before a Holy God. It is also true that justification is accomplished through no effort of our own, and when we are justified, all of our sins are forgiven. For a sinner to be "justified" means they have been divinely pardoned and legally deemed not guilty. Justification is the only way to a relationship with God. It is through a repentant heart professing faith in Jesus Christ for the remission of our sins.

When we are justified, we accept Him as the Son of God, and we acknowledge His sacrifice on the cross

68

which, in turn, paid the penalty for our sin. After we have received grace, we also receive the Holy Spirit. Thus, begins the process of sanctification, but we are not yet sanctified. While we live in our physical bodies, and as we remain in Christ, we are being sanctified. It is by the empowerment of the Holy Spirit that we are enabled and equipped to overcome the dominion of sin in our lives. Following our justification, then comes a call to holiness. We are given instructions in the Bible for things we are "to do," and we are given help from the Holy Spirit to do them. We are also sternly warned that there are consequences if we do not "remain" in Christ. The consequence of not remaining in Him is the jeopardy of our eternal position.

Peter was speaking of Paul's message and he said, *"His letters contain some things that are hard to understand, which ignorant and unstable people distort, as they do the other Scriptures, to their own destruction. Therefore, dear friends, since you have been forewarned, be on your guard **so that you may not be carried away by the error of the lawless and fall from your secure position.** But grow in the grace and knowledge of our Lord and Savior Jesus Christ."* {2 Peter 3:16-17}

The Apostle Paul explained that salvation has two components. He said it requires Lordship through the process of sanctification and faith. *"...God from the beginning chose you for **salvation <u>through</u> sanctification by the Spirit <u>and</u> belief in the truth,** to which He called you by our gospel, for the obtaining of the glory of our Lord Jesus Christ."* {2 Thes 2:13-14}

1) **Justification** = Divinely Pardoned and Legally Pronounced Not Guilty (PARDONED)

2) **Sanctification** = To Make Holy, Consecrate, Separate (PROCESS)

3) **Salvation** = Glorification, Deliverance, Safety
   (PRIZE)

To receive salvation, we must first be justified, and then as we are being sanctified, we must endure.

This was the gospel that Jesus, Paul, and Peter preached. Biblical sanctification is built upon justification. However, justification is in no way established upon sanctification. This means that we are not at all justified by our performance. Although, we also don't want to focus solely on sanctification, apart from our justification. It is not a process of professing our faith once, and then concentrating only on keeping the law or doing good deeds. We must actively die to sin by the power of the Holy Spirit and not by any merit of our own. This requires a daily and ongoing relationship with the Lord. Our minds are renewed as we meditate on God's Word. We are given spiritual understanding, and we are enabled by the Spirit of God to become obedient to His Word. Our desires are transformed because our heart is not set on the things of this world; instead, we become transformed as our minds are renewed in His Word and in His presence. The process of sanctification is empowered by the Holy Spirit working within us as we continue to cooperate with the Spirit and choose to seek first God's plans and purposes for our lives.

In contrast, if we only emphasize the grace of justification, and virtually eliminate the need to honor the Lord by doing what He has asked of us, the result is a massive disconnect from the message of the gospel. As a result, the message becomes distorted. Paul made two points in Philippians 2:12-13. First, the believer must do their part, and secondly, that the power of God's Spirit will work in us. He said, *"continue to work*

70

out your salvation with fear and trembling, for it is God who works in you to will and to act in order to fulfill his good purpose."

I was discussing this topic with a friend of mine who said, "What about the thief on the cross? He only had to believe, and Jesus said that he would be in Paradise with Him that same day?" That's right. The thief was justified at the moment he believed and professed his faith in Christ. He obtained salvation and became righteous before the Lord in that moment. However, let's remember, the thief professed his faith in his last dying breaths, so there was no opportunity for him to have wandered away at a later time. This is truly a great demonstration of God's great mercy and love.

Jesus gave a wonderful illustration, He said, *"For the kingdom of heaven is like a landowner who went out early in the morning to hire workers for his vineyard. He agreed to pay them a denarius for the day and sent them into his vineyard. "About nine in the morning he went out and saw others standing in the marketplace doing nothing. He told them, 'You also go and work in my vineyard, and I will pay you whatever is right.' So they went. "He went out again about noon and about three in the afternoon and did the same thing. About five in the afternoon he went out and found still others standing around. He asked them, 'Why have you been standing here all day long doing nothing?' "Because no one has hired us,' they answered. He said to them, 'You also go and work in my vineyard.' "When evening came, the owner of the vineyard said to his foreman, 'Call the workers and pay them their wages, beginning with the last ones hired and going on to the first.' "The workers who were hired about five in the afternoon came and each received a denarius. So **when those came who were hired first, they expected to receive more.** But each one of them also received a denarius. When they received it, **they began to***

71

grumble against the landowner. 'These who were hired last worked only one hour,' they said, 'and you have made them equal to us who have borne the burden of the work and the heat of the day. But he answered one of them, 'I am not being unfair to you, friend. Didn't you agree to work for a denarius? Take your pay and go. <u>I want to give the one who was hired last the same as I gave you. Don't I have the right to do what I want with my own money?</u> Or are you envious because I am generous?'" {Matt 20:1-16}

Even after living a full life of sin, the thief on the cross was pardoned in his last breaths. There was no chance for him to be pulled away by worldly nonsense. He was blessed indeed! But, don't let the circumstances breed confusion over the requirements of Lordship vs a stand-alone profession of faith. If the thief on the cross had more time on earth, Jesus would have told him, "Go and Sin No More" and "Remain in Me."

Ultimately, sanctification is God's work. Yet, as we cooperate with Him, He works through the sincere and self-disciplined pursuits of His people, not despite them. Justification does not discharge a believer from the requirement of obedience. In fact, the exact opposite is true. Sanctification merely means that our obedience is a Spirit-empowered work of God and that God will help us endure and overcome. But, we still have to do our part by choosing to participate with Him. My free will remains, and each day it is my choice to remain in Christ. Paul made it emphatically clear that there is only one true gospel. He boldly embraced the assignment he had been given by the Lord, when he said, *"...I am appointed for the defense of the gospel."* {Phil 1:16}

When he was addressing the Galatian churches he said that if anyone, *"...preach any other gospel to you*

than what we have preached to you, let him be accursed."
{Gal 1:8}

Paul also tells us that there was a secret that had been hidden, but it was now being revealed to all of God's people through the message of the gospel. *"God has given me the responsibility of serving his church by proclaiming his entire message to you. This message was kept secret for centuries and generations past, but now it has been revealed to God's people. For God wanted them to know that the riches and glory of Christ are for you Gentiles, too. And this is the secret: Christ lives in you."* {Col 1:25-27}

The secret which Paul spoke of was actually the New Covenant that God made with His people. The prophet Ezekiel told how the New Covenant would be fulfilled. He said, *"I will give you a new heart and put a new spirit in you; I will remove from you your heart of stone and give you a heart of flesh. And I will put my Spirit in you and move you to follow my decrees and be careful to keep my laws."* {Ezekiel 36:26-27 NIV}

In the Old Testament, the people of God did not have the Holy Spirit dwelling inside of them. This was true unless the Lord intentionally placed His Spirit upon someone. Throughout Paul's ministry, he made it clear that apart from Christ, there is no justification. He emphasized that justification cannot be gained merely by keeping the law itself. But, he was also clear that it is because of the law that we know right from wrong. *"Therefore, by the deeds of the law no flesh will be justified in His sight, for by the law is the knowledge of sin."* {Romans 3:20}

*"Therefore, we conclude that a man is **justified by faith apart from the deeds of the law.**"* {Rom 3:28}

Notice the word used in this verse from Romans 3:28 "justified," which means being pronounced "not guilty." It is only after justification by faith that we can move into the process of sanctification. Sanctification is built upon our justification in Christ.

The Lord's motive in establishing the process of sanctification is intended to lead us towards righteousness as we grow closer in our relationship with Him. He wants us to realize the depths of His love for us. Everything He has instructed us to do is for our good and our benefit. He wants us to love Him so much that we will long to follow Him and keep His commands.

Writing to Roman Christians, Paul said, *"What then? **Shall we sin because we are not under law but under grace? Certainly not!** Do you not know that to whom you present yourselves slaves to obey, you are that one's slaves whom you obey, **whether of sin leading to death, or of obedience leading to righteousness**? But God be thanked that though you were slaves of sin, yet you obeyed from the heart that form of doctrine to which you were delivered. **And having been set free from sin, you became slaves of righteousness**. I speak in human terms because of the weakness of your flesh. For just as you presented your members as slaves of uncleanness, and of lawlessness leading to more lawlessness, so **now present your members as slaves of righteousness for holiness.***" {Rom 6:15-19}

He is asking these Roman Christians whether or not they understand that we must actively participate in this process of sanctification. We must present ourselves daily to the Lord and seek His will because we are now under His Lordship. Based on what the Bible actually says, those who believe or promote a gospel message of faith with no additional requirements are promoting a false gospel. There IS a requirement after our profession of faith, and this requirement is not to be missed. The requirement is Lordship.

We must "remain in Christ" to receive salvation. Because we are merely human, we are not capable of living righteously, apart from Christ. We must choose this day, and every day, whom we will serve. Jesus said, *"No one can serve two masters; for either he will hate the one and love the other, or else he will be loyal to the one and despise the other."* {Matt 6:24}

We have established that it is by faith alone that we are justified. Our justification then leads to Lordship, and Lordship enables us to be sanctified. Sanctification is the process of our being made Holy through righteous living and pursuits. Our sanctification is enabled and empowered by and through the Holy Spirit.

So, the question remains, can salvation be lost if the Lordship of Jesus Christ is abandoned? If we trade Lordship for self-gratification and worldly pursuits, and if we never repent or return to a right relationship with Christ, have we actually endured? After all, it was Jesus Himself who said, *"But **he who endures** to the end shall be saved."* {Matt 24:13}

The deception of eternal security began in the Garden of Eden. Satan has always been an unrelenting adversary. Let's not forget that He doesn't come with horns and a pitchfork. He comes as an angel of light. Do you remember what he told Eve? Here's your apple. He reasoned with Eve and caused her to doubt what God said about eating from the tree. He intimated that she had misunderstood what God instructed. Now, we all know that Eve would not have gone hungry had she not eaten from that one tree. God had provided all that she and Adam needed. In return, He only had one command for them, *"You are free to eat from any tree in the garden; but you must not eat from the tree of the knowledge of good and evil, for when you eat from it you will certainly die."* {Gen 2:16-17}

That snake's sole mission was to cause Eve to mistrust God and to confound His Words. In fact, the first lie Satan told a human being was, effectively, the same issue that we're talking about right now. He was trying to get Eve to dismiss an eternal truth. Eve knew she would be disobeying God's commands, but the serpent lied to her and said, *"You will not surely die."*

".... He said to the woman, "Did God really say, 'You must not eat from any tree in the garden'?" The woman said to the serpent, "We may eat fruit from the trees in the garden, but God did say, 'You must not eat fruit from the tree that is in the middle of the garden, and you must not touch it, or you will die.' "You will not certainly die," the serpent said to the woman. {Gen 3:1-4}

The saga continues through the generations. For us, the deception sounds like this, "Did God really say you must endure? Didn't God say that all you need to do is believe, once and for all, and then nothing else is required? Did God really mean that we are to become a slave to righteousness instead of our old sinful ways? Didn't He know that we could never be righteous? Isn't that why He went to the cross?"

Jesus told us what will happen if we don't stay with Him in this process of sanctification. He has made it clear that we have a choice. ***"Remain in me, as I also remain in you. No branch can bear fruit by itself; it must remain in the vine.*** *Neither can you bear fruit unless you remain in me.* ***I am the vine; you are the branches.*** *If you remain in me and I in you, you will bear much fruit; apart from me you can do nothing.* ***If you do not remain in me, you are like a branch that is thrown away*** *and* *withers; such branches are picked up, thrown into the fire and burned."* {John 15:4-11}

Surely, Jesus didn't really mean it like that. Did He really say that if we don't remain in Him, we will be thrown into the fire? He absolutely did. Don't listen to the counterfeit voices of Satan and the foolishness of our secular society. Recognize the voice of the enemy questioning God's Word. Avoid those who study only half of the Bible and discount the other half. It is God's Word alone that gives us spiritual truth. Any other path will lead us astray. "

...For we are not unaware of his schemes." {2 Cor 2:11}

If there is anything that Satan will make every effort to thwart, it is the one true gospel of Christ. He is relentless as he works to steer the multitudes away from the narrow path. He wants us to ignore the truth that leads us to repentance, grace through Christ, sanctification and a saving faith that endures. What about the great commission? This is the true gospel according to Jesus, and in it, He instructs us to act after we have placed our faith in Him. He says, *"Go therefore and make disciples of all the nations, baptizing them in the name of the Father and of the Son and of the Holy Spirit, **teaching them to observe all things that I have commanded you;** and lo, I am with you always, even to the end of the age."* {Matt 28:19-20}

In the Bible, we find many parallels between our relationship with God and marriage. God frequently uses the illustration of marriage to help us understand the type of relationship He wants to have with us, as well as the depth of His love. Marriage is a sacred commitment, and it is one that is not to be taken lightly. Jesus gave only two justifications for which divorce would be permissible and not counted as sin. The Lord said that if an unbelieving spouse departs, let them go. The only other reason is adultery. {1 Cor 7:15 and Matt 5:32; 19:9}

It does not surprise me at all that God would not require a faithful spouse to remain bound to a person who violates the purity of the relationship. When a spouse is unfaithful, they have trampled the vows of their covenant relationship. They have counted their sacred union as a common thing. This concept reminds me of a challenging Scripture, *"Of how much worse punishment, do you suppose, will he be thought worthy who has trampled the Son of God underfoot, counted the blood of the* **covenant _by which he was sanctified_ a common thing, and insulted the Spirit of grace?** *For we know Him who said, "Vengeance is Mine, I will repay," says the Lord. And again, "The Lord will judge His people." It is a fearful thing to fall into the hands of the living God."* {Heb 10:29-31}

Can you hear the heartbreak and anger as Paul refers to one of the Lord's sons or daughters who has turned their back on the Lord? Betrayal, after having acknowledged the sacrifice made on their behalf, and after having received a full pardon. Despite the gentle promptings of the Holy Spirit, they turn back to their own self-seeking desires and choose a pleasure-loving course. This person has obviously given no reverence or consideration to the seriousness of the commitment they made when, by faith, they accepted Christ and gave Him Lordship over their lives. In the same way, the heart of a faithful spouse is broken by the betrayal of an unfaithful husband or wife who violates the covenant relationship. Such actions make the solemn vows made before friends, family, and God seem like words without value.

We generally think of an idol as a statue, but an idol is anything that we put before our relationship with God. Just as our husband or wife will not allow another person to be placed before them in our marital relationship, neither will God allow anyone or anything else to become more important or exalted than our relationship with Him. Remaining in Christ stems from the attitude of our heart; it is not just knowing about Him. It is an active love relationship. Throughout the Bible, we see demonstrations of God's faithfulness. God was faithful even when His people were not faithful to Him. In the Old Testament, we learn how He pleaded with the Israelites to repent and return to Him before it was too late for reconciliation. If we have breath in us, then there is still hope for us. The Lord is patiently waiting for those who have gone down the broad path (which leads to destruction) to come to their senses, repent and return to Him with all of their heart. In Greek, the word for remain is 'menó,' which means to stay.

The Lord gave us a New Covenant to replace the Old Covenant. The New Covenant would equip God's people by indwelling us with His Holy Spirit, so we would be enabled to keep His commands. However, keep in mind that the Lord does not change. We are advised to obey God's laws. Would you like to know how the Bible defines the love of God? *"For this is the love of God, that we keep His commandments."* {1 John 5:3}

It is through both the Old and New Testaments that we begin to understand God's character and His intentions. *"I the LORD do not change."* {Mal 3:6}

Do you realize that you can be walking north and not be walking true north? On a compass there are actually two norths, but each one will not lead us to the same destination. There is a magnetic north and a true north. We need to be absolutely certain we are heading true north... our eternal destination may depend on it. *Jesus said, "Everyone who hears these words of Mine and does not act on them, will be like a foolish man who built his house on the sand."* {Matt 7:26}

Let's make sure we are heading true north!

CHAPTER FIVE

Gospel of Accommodation

"Examine yourselves to see whether you are in the faith; test yourselves. Do you not realize that Christ Jesus is in you — unless, of course, you fail the test?" {2 Cor 13:5 NIV}

Many corporations hire internal auditors as full-time employees. The primary role of the auditor is to self-examine the company on a regular basis so they can be sure everything remains in order, just in case the I.R.S comes calling. When was the last time you conducted an audit measuring yourself by the standards we find in Gods Word?

Principally, being Christian is about love and where you direct your love. So, if you're saved, you love the Lord. This is the first test. If you genuinely love the Lord, you will desire to glorify Him. You will want to learn more about Him. You will enjoy talking about Him. Because His Spirit lives in you, you will seek to honor Him and Praise His Holy name. You will begin to feel uncomfortable around the things that offend the Lord. He will gently let you know when something doesn't line up with who He has called you to be. Do you know why you believe what you believe? Our perspectives as well as our beliefs have been forged by our experiences, our upbringing, an influential person(s) or a doctrine. We are all products of our environment and influences.

Regardless of what we choose to believe, the absolute truth never changes. Many people believe there are no absolute truths. However, to say there is no absolute truth is, in fact, an absolute truth. Let me give you an example. You could stand at the edge of the ocean, close your eyes, and tell yourself that the waves will not continue to roll onto the shore. And, we both know that your feet are going to get wet because what you choose to believe will not change what is true. The Word of God says to *"...work out your own salvation with fear and trembling;* {Phil 2:12}

All Scripture gives us one clear message: God is God, and we are not. Therefore, we need to align ourselves with Him. The one thing that we can all agree on is that none of us will be getting out of here alive, unless Jesus rolls back the clouds while we are still breathing. So, this is a big deal. We need to be sure we understand what His Word says. Otherwise, we might be in for a shock on the day we stand before His throne. We should uplift and magnify the grace of God, and we should recognize the role of grace in our salvation. However, in our pursuit of the truth, we should also seek the fullness of biblical revelation and not set one component of it over and against all the rest. The Bible warned that there would come a time when the gospel would be perverted. It says that in the last days, men will be lovers of pleasure instead of lovers of God. Scripture foretold that people would not want to hear anything that rebukes their lusts or sinful course.

Allow me to introduce the gospel of accommodation. The churches who support this doctrine will be comfortable and non-offensive.

They will encourage the lost to simply come to the cross and say, "Yes, Lord I believe." They will say that you can receive all the benefits of the cross and even go back to your blatant sinful ways, all because you've received salvation by faith, and by faith alone. There is no teaching about dying to our past sins and living a new life that is transformed by Christ. That is the offense of the cross. When you come to the cross, it requires that you go all the way. It is not only the saving of the soul, it is also the saving of the body. The Lord wants our bodies as a living sacrifice. Yes, I will give you a verse for that. He died to overcome the dominion of sin in our lives. If the message of grace doesn't have righteousness as its ultimate objective, it is a misleading and different gospel. *"For the grace of God has been revealed, bringing salvation to all people. **And we are instructed to turn from godless living and sinful pleasures.** We should live in this evil world with wisdom, righteousness, and devotion to God, while we look forward with hope to that wonderful day when the glory of our great God and Savior, Jesus Christ, will be revealed."* {Titus 2:11-13 NLT}

*"I beseech you therefore, brethren, by the mercies of God, that you **present your bodies a living sacrifice,** holy, acceptable to God, which is your reasonable service. **And do not be conformed to this world, but be transformed by the renewing of your mind,** that you may prove what is that good and acceptable and perfect will of God."* {Rom 12:1-2}

The eternal Word of God is the source of our salvation. How can we be so sure that the Word of God is the Truth? Because the Word of God is God.

- *"In the beginning was the Word, and the Word was with God, **and the Word was God.**"* {John 1:1}

- *"Sanctify them in the truth; your word is truth."* {John 17:17}

- *"Your word is a lamp to my feet and a light to my path."* {Psalm 119:105}

- *"And the Word became flesh and dwelt among us..."* {John 1:14}

I often hear people questioning the Bible. Some dismiss its validity because of the number of translations, and some question why there were other books of the Bible that were left out? So, here is my response: God is sovereign and in control. Do you really think that the God who created the universe and everything in it, is not capable of ensuring the Bible would turn out and be held together in the exact way He intended it to? That is essentially what it means to say that God is sovereign and in control, He is able. If there was a book left out, then I believe it was because God did not intend for it to be included. *"For God is not the author of confusion..."* {1 Cor 14:33} Of course, the devil would love nothing more than to cause you to mistrust the Word of God.

I've spent a lot of time thoughtfully considering the statements of faith from those who profess eternal security or "Once Saved, Always Saved." There is a well-known and very respected pastor who teaches this doctrine. He has a significant global ministry, and I like many of his messages. But on this important piece of theology, we wholeheartedly disagree. As the Holy Spirit began revealing truths to me, I spent a lot of time earnestly studying in Scripture.

At times, I seriously questioned whether I was discerning the Bible accurately, in part it was because this respected minister had an opposing opinion. To this day, I consider him to be a devout man of God who is committed to the faith. So, I thought, could I be wrong? How could the Holy Spirit be revealing something entirely different to me? In my research, I also found another well-respected minister with an equally sizable global ministry who shares the same convictions that I do. So, how is it that two well-known and respected ministers of the Lord (who preach from the same Bible) would teach opposing theologies. Obviously, one of these views is in error. Ultimately, and after much prayer, I am resolved that what any man has to say in contradiction of God's Word, should be entirely ignored.

What truly matters is that we have diligently and personally sought the Lord and that we humbly submit ourselves to guidance by the Holy Spirit. We are instructed that we should not rely solely on a man to teach us. Instead, through prayer and discernment, we are to seek the truth in God's Word. In doing so, the Holy Spirit will give us knowledge and understanding.

Once we've heard a few Scriptures on salvation over and over, we might feel confident that we know all that the Bible teaches on salvation. After all, our favorite pastor may have emphatically told us that our salvation cannot be lost. He may have preached boldly to the congregation, saying that all one needs to do is to believe in Christ. He may assure his followers that there is no other requirement in order to maintain our eternal security. Surely, this pastor went to seminary, and he is loved and respected by so many. He can't possibly be wrong, can he?

"You believe that there is one God. You do well. Even the demons believe—and tremble! But do you want to know, O

foolish man, that faith without works is dead?" {James 2:19-20}

Faith is something that you do. A believer is not someone that has merely accepted facts. Becoming a genuine believer involves trusting in Jesus, not just knowing about Jesus. Trusting is something that we do. The apostle James taught about a good man named Abraham and a bad woman named Rahab, and he said that both were justified by what they "did." *"And so it happened just as the Scriptures say: "Abraham believed God, and God counted him as righteous because of his faith." He was even called the friend of God. **So you see, we are shown to be right with God by what we do, not by faith alone.** Rahab the prostitute is another example. **She was shown to be right with God by her actions** when she hid those messengers and sent them safely away by a different road. Just as the body is dead without breath, so also faith is dead without good works."* {James 2:23-25 NLT}

The question we must ask ourselves is this, despite what some of our favorite pastors believe, are we willing to gamble our souls on anything other than what the Bible actually teaches? There are numerous opposing beliefs, and all of them are not correct, regardless of who is touting them. There are many astute words and logical arguments spewed to the masses, but the Truth comes from only one source. The Holy Spirit will speak to us through God's Word.

*"As for you, the anointing you received from him remains in you, and **you do not need anyone to teach you.** But as **his anointing teaches you about all things and as that anointing is real, not counterfeit**—just as it has taught you, **remain in him.**"* {1 John 2:27 NIV}

"I tell you this so that no one may deceive you by fine-sounding arguments." {Col 2:4 -NIV}

We are saved only by grace through faith, but it is our works that demonstrate the sincerity of our faith. For this reason, many passages teach that God will judge all humanity by our actions. Without exception, *"He will render to each one according to his works: to those who by patience in well-doing seek for glory and honor and immortality, he will give eternal life; **but for those who are self-seeking and do not obey the truth, but obey un-righteousness,** there will be wrath and fury."* {Rom 2:6-11}

To believe in perseverance does not negate that repentance through faith in Christ alone, justifies and brings us into a righteous position with God. The act of perseverance actually affirms our faith. Principally, we should not presume that we've spiritually arrived and are outside the bounds of Scripture's warnings. Instead, *"be all the more diligent to make your calling and election sure, for **if you practice these qualities you will never fall.**"* {2 Pet. 1:10}

*"Don't be fooled by those who try to excuse these sins, for the anger of God will fall on all who disobey him…So be careful how you live. Don't live like fools, but like those who are wise. Make the most of every opportunity in these evil days. Don't act thoughtlessly, but **understand what the Lord wants you to do.**"* {Ephesians 5:6;15-17 NLT}

I believe there are a number of Christian leaders who would agree that as it relates to God's Word, it is probably not the best idea to solely seek validation in the area that satisfies our personal preferences or position on a given topic. Wisdom seeks truth, regardless of the answer. Fundamentally, here is what it means to know the truth, *"…Jesus said to the people who believed in him, "You are truly my disciples **if you remain faithful to my teachings.** And you will know the truth, and the truth will set you free."* {John 8:31-32 NLT}

The pride of human wisdom and the ignorance, or even contempt, for the influence of the Holy Spirit, have caused professing Christians and even those who teach others, to turn away from the requirements of God.

"My people are destroyed for lack of knowledge." {Hosea 4:6}

Paul boldly declared the need to defend the true gospel, *"Preach the word; be prepared in season and out of season; correct, rebuke and encourage—with great patience and careful instruction. For the time will come when people will not put up with sound doctrine. Instead, to suit their own desires, they will gather around them a great number of teachers to say what their itching ears want to hear. They will turn their ears away from the truth and turn aside to myths."* {2 Tim 4:2-4 NIV}

Paul was not referring to the non-religious. He is referencing the professing Christians who make inclination their guide. Inclination is a person's natural tendency, to act or to feel a particular way because they are consumed by self-desires. These are people who will only listen to a doctrine that doesn't condemn or require an adjustment to their pleasure-loving course. They are offended by the plain words of truth as they are delivered by the bold and faithful followers of Christ, and so they choose teachers who only encourage them with words of affirmation and tolerance. In our society today, it is more and more common to hear professing ministers preach opinions of men, instead of the Word of God. In all actuality, by ignoring the Word of God, they are leading those who look to them for spiritual guidance astray. As followers of Christ, we are now called to holiness. The Bible says that if we reject this call to holiness, we are not rejecting man;

instead, we are actually rejecting God. *"For God did not call us to be impure, but to live a holy life. Therefore, anyone who rejects this instruction does not reject a human being but God, the very God who gives you his Holy Spirit."* {1 Thess 4:7-8 NIV}

We can reject God by ignoring the conviction of the Holy Spirit and exalting our own desires over the pursuit of righteousness in Christ. This verse affirms that we can absolutely reject God after receiving salvation. Jesus spoke to the religious leaders, *"Woe to you, teachers of the law and Pharisees, you hypocrites! You shut the door of the kingdom of heaven in people's faces. You yourselves do not enter, nor will you let those enter who are trying to. "Woe to you, teachers of the law and Pharisees, you hypocrites! You travel over land and sea to win a single convert, and when you have succeeded, you make them twice as much a child of hell as you are...In the same way, on the outside you appear to people as righteous but on the inside you are full of hypocrisy and wickedness."* {Matt 23:13-15;28 NIV}

The Pharisees and the Sadducees were both religious sects within Judaism during the time of Christ. Both groups honored Moses and the law, and both had a measure of political power. Some have interpreted this verse as if Jesus was actually condemning the law. His tone in the writing seems hostile as He rebukes the Pharisees as "teachers of the law." But, as we further examine Jesus' position on the law, we will discover that He was not condemning the law. In fact, in Matthew 5:17-19, Jesus said that not one pen stroke of the Old Testament law would be changed until heaven and earth pass away. Jesus told the religious leaders that because of their hypocrisy, He would Himself be sending prophets, wise men and teachers of religious law. {Matt 23:34}

"Do not think that I have come to abolish the Law or the Prophets; I have not come to abolish them but to fulfill them. For truly I tell you **until heaven and earth disappear**, *not the smallest letter,* **not the least stroke of a pen, will by any means disappear from the Law until everything is accomplished.** *Therefore,* **anyone who sets aside one of the least of these commands and teaches others accordingly will be called least in the kingdom of heaven**, *but whoever practices and teaches these commands will be called great in the kingdom of heaven."* {Matt 5:17-19}

Jesus was condemning the Pharisees because, at best, they were misleading people with their misinterpretation and misunderstanding of the Scriptures. At worst, the Pharisees were "twisting" the Scriptures to satisfy their own interests. And, it is still happening today. *"For those who guide this people are leading them astray; And those who are guided by them are brought to confusion."* {Isaiah 9:16}

Most people today want an easy religion. They dwell solely on the love of Jesus. Ignoring the clarity of Scripture on topics like salvation and endurance can lead to a counterfeit experience for many professing Christians. It is also a great danger to the many who are not opening their Bibles to validate that what they are being taught is actually the truth. At my church, our associate pastor gave a sermon on gentleness. He explained that for us to fully understand the gentleness of God, he would need to share other Scriptures that would help us understand the power and might of our God as well. He said that we need to look at the whole picture to have an accurate understanding. Only then, he contended, could we grasp the fullness and the true meaning of the message. The point he was making was that God is gentle, but it's not because He is weak. The Bible teaches that He can literally pick up the entire earth. He commands the winds and the sea. We see His wrath demonstrated towards sin in ancient times, and we know that the judgment of God is coming upon the whole earth at the end of time. However, in His gentleness towards us, He shows complete restraint by His own choice. Yet, He is full of might and power. Think of the restraint required while He was on the cross. As He hung there, He was mocked and ridiculed. The soldiers said to Him, *"Well then, save yourself and come down from the cross!"* {Mark 15:30} Of course, He could have come down. He could have proven Himself. But in gentleness and love, He demonstrated full restraint by staying on the cross for us. Fundamentally, in order for one to be considered gentle, one would also need to have power over something or someone, much like a tamed Lion. The point here is that if you don't seek to discover the truth from all sides, you risk misunderstanding the truth altogether.

When we learn something from anyone that is teaching from Scripture, it is always a good practice to go back to our Bible and read the entire chapter. In this way, we will gain the context of what is being said. If a portion of a verse is omitted, it can change its meaning entirely. Omission can allow doctrine to be twisted and taught incorrectly. For example, I mentioned a verse from John 8:31-32 earlier. Whether you realize it or not, you are probably familiar with the latter part of the verse because it is frequently used in both sermons and speeches. *"And you shall know the truth, and the truth shall set you free."*

That is an awesome truth. But, if we ignore the first part of the verse, it allows room for confusion. This verse begins with, *"**If** you abide in my Word..."* Once again with the promise, comes a condition. Though we don't always like it, in order to obtain the promise, you must first comply with the condition. So, let's put it all together, *"If you abide in my word... you shall know the truth, and the truth shall set you free."* If you leave off the first part, then one can infer that I just need to find the truth, and I'll be free. The actual message from this verse states that if we are to find the truth, we must "abide" in the Word of God.

Speaking of finding the truth...Accepting Jesus into our hearts as the son of God is not a license to sin. We are forgiven for all future sins **when we "repent"** of our wrongs. We were not automatically forgiven for all future sins with no expectation of future repentance. Our sanctification is an ongoing process of spiritual growth and repentance. We will not be condemned by sin if we are walking according to the Spirit. When the Holy Spirit reveals that a person is living sinfully, and that person ignores the conviction and continues in the sinful lifestyle, they are not walking according to the Spirit. They have made a choice to walk according to the flesh. Salvation is not a calling to perfection. It is a call to repentance, to obedience and submission to Jesus Christ as Lord over our lives. God is not calling us to a theology. He is inviting us to a personal relationship with Him. But, He has made it clear that the relationship will only work if we will deny ourselves and enthrone Him as Lord. The Bible teaches that the fear of the Lord is the greatest deterrent against sin. *"Moses said to the people, "Do not be afraid. God has come to test you so that the fear of God will be with you to keep you from sinning."* {Exodus 20:20}

Most Christians don't want to talk about things like "fearing" God. I recently had a conversation with a Christian friend of mine on the topic of eternal security. His position was that it's not good to use fear to convince someone about God or about salvation. He said, "Some people already have issues with authority, and they view God as out to get them." I am sure that it would not surprise you that I believe we should not present a "watered down" version of the truth. The Word of God is truth, and the truth will be revealed by the Spirit when we faithfully teach the entire Word. We shouldn't shy away from teaching the fullness of the Word for fear of being rejected by man. I believe we should cloak the truth in gentleness and love, but we need to have the courage to speak God's Word. We live in a dying world and a corrupt generation that needs followers of Jesus who will be bold enough to tell them the truth, even at the risk of being persecuted.

- *"And on some have compassion, making a distinction; **but others save with fear, pulling them out of the fire,** hating even the garment defiled by the flesh."* {Jude 22}

- *"Through love and faithfulness sin is atoned for; through the fear of the Lord, evil is avoided."* {Prov 16:6}

Those who view God solely as a kind and loving grandfather may have a casual view on sin and may worship half-heartedly. They are more likely to live on their own terms. It is not my intent to instill fear simply for the sake of instilling fear. Fear is a matter that is terribly misunderstood as it relates to the Lord.

*"The **fear of the Lord** is the **beginning of wisdom** and the knowledge of the Holy One is understanding."* {Prov 9:10}

Things like "fearing God" and the concept of "eternal security" rile many Christians. In fact, my flesh really does not want to fight about the topic of eternal security. Part of me would prefer to quietly let everyone believe whatever they choose to believe. Maybe I should just move along as if it's none of my business. However, I believe the Holy Spirit has put a fiery passion in my soul for the people that need to hear the truth. He has confirmed His will for me time and time again. This is a topic I have been passionate about for years, but I feel a sense of urgency like never before, and I intend to humbly point to the Word of God, so we can all gain understanding.

Let's be honest, it's much more appealing to the masses when a non-threatening image of the Lord is presented. It's easier to market Christianity when we present a singular view of Jesus as a kind and loving shepherd watching over His flock. Today, our society is obsessed with its own comfort. But, I firmly believe that we do a dis-service to ourselves and to new Christians when we downplay, or ignore, the importance of a healthy fear of the Lord, as well as the reverence and intentional commitment of our time that a relationship with Him requires.

- *"How blessed is the man who fears always,"* {Prov 28:14}

- *"And His mercy is on those who fear Him From generation to generation."* {Luke 1:50}

- *"The LORD takes pleasure in those who fear Him, in those who hope in His mercy."* {Psalm 147:11}

- *"Surely His salvation is near to those who fear Him,"* {Psalm 85:9}

Our world does not promote fear of anything, including God. But as it relates to the Lord, it is wise to fear Him. Reverence and awe of the Lord encourage us to remain steadfast. As a true believer, indwelt by the Holy Spirit, He enables us to walk in love, joy, and a sound mind. He liberates us from the fear of man. He frees us from fear of anything in the physical realm. When we belong to Christ, the only thing we need to fear is Him. It is a healthy fear. A healthy fear of God is like the feeling that a child has when he is considering a willful act of disobedience. Even at a young age, that child will consider the consequences of disobeying his parent. Even though the child knows he is loved, he also learns there are consequences for disobedience. As we know, it is discipline that drives the child away from harmful choices. It is no different for Christians in our relationship with our heavenly Father.

A deep sense of awe is vital to truly knowing God.

"Who has measured the waters in the hollow of his hand, or with the breadth of his hand marked off the heavens? Who has held the dust of the earth in a basket, or weighed the mountains on the scales and the hills in a balance? Who can fathom the Spirit of the LORD, or instruct the LORD as his counselor? Whom did the LORD consult to enlighten him, and who taught him the right way? Who was it that taught him knowledge, or showed him the path of understanding? Surely the nations are like a drop in a bucket; they are regarded as dust on the scales; he weighs the islands as though they were fine dust. Lebanon is not sufficient for altar fires, nor its animals enough for burnt offerings. Before him all the nations are as nothing; they are regarded by him as worthless and less than nothing. With whom, then, will you compare God? To what image will you liken him? As for an idol, a metalworker casts it, and a goldsmith overlays it with gold and fashions silver chains for it. A person too poor to present such an offering selects wood that will not rot; they look for a skilled worker to set up an idol that will not topple. Do you not know? Have you not heard? Has it not been told you from the beginning? Have you not understood since the earth was founded? He sits enthroned above the circle of the earth, and its people are like grasshoppers. He stretches out the heavens like a canopy and spreads them

out like a tent to live in. He brings princes to naught and reduces the rulers of this world to nothing. No sooner are they planted, no sooner are they sown, no sooner do they take root in the ground than he blows on them and they wither, and a whirlwind sweeps them away like chaff. "To whom will you compare me? Or who is my equal?" says the Holy One. Lift up your eyes and look to the heavens: Who created all these? He who brings out the starry host one by one and calls forth each of them by name. Because of his great power and mighty strength, not one of them is missing." {Isaiah 40:12-26 NIV}

Our Creator is mighty and powerful. He is gentle. He is jealous. He is a vengeful God. He is a God full of mercy and grace. His love is lavish. He defends His children. He is a strong tower and a mighty fortress. He is a comforter. He is full of love and slow to anger. There is no one and nothing like Him. He is the Savior of those who call upon His name and submit to His Lordship. He is worthy to be praised. His name is to be revered, and He is to be feared from generation to generation. He is a Holy God. He is the same God of yesterday, today and forever, He does not change. He is faithful! *"As for you, see that what you have heard from the beginning remains in you. **If it does,** you also will remain in the Son and in the Father. And this is what he promised us—eternal life."* {1 John 2:24-25}

The Bible says that our flesh and our spirit will always be in opposition. *"For the flesh desires what is contrary to the Spirit, and the Spirit what is contrary to the flesh. They are in conflict with each other so that **you are not to do whatever you want.**"* {Gal 5:17} We do not get better because we get spiritual. As we learn to live and submit ourselves to the guidance of the Spirit, the flesh and its desires are put away.

We can learn from King David's example, he prayed:

96

"Who can understand his errors? Cleanse me from secret faults. Keep back Your servant also from presumptuous sins; Let them not have dominion over me. Then I shall be blameless, And I shall be innocent of great transgression. Let the words of my mouth and the meditation of my heart Be acceptable in Your sight, O LORD, my strength and my Redeemer." {Psalms 19:12-14}

CHAPTER SIX

Did God Really Say That?

*"So **why do you keep calling me 'Lord, Lord!' when you don't do what I say?** I will show you what it's like when someone comes to me, listens to my teaching, and then follows it. It is like a person building a house who digs deep and lays the foundation on solid rock. When the floodwaters rise and break against that house, it stands firm because it is well built. **But anyone who hears and doesn't obey** is like a person who builds a house right on the ground, without a foundation. When the floods sweep down against that house, it will collapse into a heap of ruins."* {Luke 6:46-49 NLT}

Jesus is passionately explaining that following Him means actually doing what He says. It requires us to take a conscious action. But, it is our choice. We have free will. He is not forcing us to listen. He is just pleading with each of us for our own good. *But Jesus said to him, "No one, having put his hand to the plow, and looking back, is fit for the kingdom of God."* {Luke 9:62}

Putting your hand to the plow represents an intentional effort to work for the benefit of God's Kingdom, in both your heart and mind. We don't need a seminary degree to share our testimony. We should be ministering to the lost and feeding the homeless. It is incumbent on us to care for the helpless and to cheer the brokenhearted. We should be steadfast in prayer for our family and friends. Others should know us by our fruits. Plowing for the Kingdom of God is the most important thing we can do with our life. Activities that produce eternal value are perhaps the most significant and worthwhile endeavors we can pursue. How much of our time and energy do we spend on things that will have served no meaningful purpose when we come to the end of our life on this earth? It was all for what? Anything that does not have an eternal value is meaningless. King Solomon, a King who was blessed with excessive wealth and wisdom, shared the same sentiment. He starts the book of Ecclesiastes like this: "...*Utterly meaningless! Everything is meaningless. What do people gain from all their labors at which they toil under the sun? Generations come and generations go...*" {Ecc 1:2-3}

I have recently started researching my ancestry online, and based on my findings, I've started building my family tree. So far, I've managed to trace "my people" back to the 1600's. It is very fascinating. As I was looking at my fairly large tree with all of its branches, it occurred to me how quickly life comes and goes. There are many layers of people on my family's tree, and after researching several of their lives, I've found that some of them were pretty impressive. But, only the people on the bottom couple of branches are still alive. Everyone else is gone, and one day I, too, will be just a memory on someone's family tree. Life is short. The Bible says our life is like a mist; we are here today and gone tomorrow, we are just a vapor. We need to realize how important it is that we wholeheartedly follow the Lord while we have the opportunity.

No turning back. However, if somehow, we find ourselves in that place where we not only look back, but perhaps even return to our former ways of life, the

Lord is full of mercy towards us. But, we must remember that He extends mercy only when we repent and return to Him. It is when we are broken and humbled that we most easily realize that He is all we need.

During my late twenties, there was a period of time when I was extremely close to the Lord. I journaled my thoughts and prayers. I would regularly pray and ask God to speak to me through His Word, and then I would randomly open the Bible to find my eyes looking at a passage of Scripture that I knew He had intended for me to read in that very moment. I had a particular room in my house that I would go to when I journaled or read my Bible. When I was in that room taking time to be alone with the Lord, I could literally feel the presence of the God with me. I could not wait to be there at some point every day. I have a verse framed in my office, and it says, "Whom shall I send... Here am I, send me!" I used to look at that verse and tell the Lord that I wanted to be that person. "Use me," I would say. I felt like I would have done whatever He asked me to do. He was first in every aspect of my life, no matter what. I was in love with Jesus. I still am... but there was a time in my life that something changed.

Looking back, I realize that the Lord allowed me to experience a time of sifting. I believe that He wanted to test my heart and my faith. I never stopped loving the Lord. It was a slow fade. It didn't happen suddenly or overnight, and honestly, I didn't even notice that it was happening. I would have never believed that I could have wandered away from Him. But, I did. I stopped journaling. I became busy with life, and I no longer made time to be with the Lord or to talk with Him about what was going on throughout my day. I would still go to church once in a while, and I always loved to hear a good sermon on the radio. I still had good intentions in my heart. I was kind to people and still set out to do "good things" for others but pursuing Him and His purposes were no longer my priority. I didn't have time for Him because I was busy with my life. I had a lot of friends, and I was having fun. I was really just going through the motions and living life my way, pursuing my own plans and building my own kingdom.

Several years later, I distinctly remember myself pondering how I ended up with a life that was so far removed from the relationship with God that I once treasured. Spiritually, I knew that I was in a dangerous place, and I prayed and asked God to help restore me. I was genuinely sorry as I realized that I had put so many other things before Him. I prayed about it, but I didn't feel compelled to do things much differently. Although I did begin hosting Bible studies at my home again, but the truth is that my heart really wasn't in it. I was trying to hold myself accountable so I would get back into God's Word. I figured that if I made a commitment to other people, then I would study and prepare so I wouldn't let them down. How sad is that? I needed a responsibility to other people, so I would remain faithful to be in God's Word. For some reason, I just wasn't motivated enough to be consistent and do it on my own.

Over the next few years, the Lord was drawing me back. I continued to meet with my group and learn from the Bible, and I noticed the Lord strengthening me. In the first chapter of this book, you may recall that I mentioned a turning point. I experienced a time of true repentance. I was at a Bible conference, and I was overwhelmed with Godly sorrow. It was as if a veil had been removed from my eyes, and I could clearly see my life story. Even though I had gone my own way in life, I could also see that God had never left me. He had been silent until I decided to seek Him again. But, He was a loving father to me. I felt like a prodigal daughter who had just run home into the arms of a merciful and loving dad. I felt His presence again in a mighty way, and I wept my heart out. It was at that moment that I knew, without any hesitation, that I had to change my life once and for all. I had to stop doing the things that were separating me from my relationship with the Lord. I had to choose Him above everything else. He was reminding me that I must remain in Him. There is no greater joy!

*Then one said to Him, "**Lord, are there few who are saved?**" And He said to them, "**Strive to enter through the narrow gate, for many, I say to you, will seek to enter and will not be able.** When once the Master of the house has risen up and shut the door, and you begin to stand outside and knock at the door, saying, 'Lord, Lord, open for us,' and He will answer and say to you, 'I do not know you, where you are from,' then you will begin to say, 'We ate and drank in Your presence, and You taught in our streets.' But He will say, 'I tell you I do not know you, where you are from. Depart from Me, all you workers of iniquity."* {Luke 13:23-27}

There is a nuance in what Jesus said, and we shouldn't miss it. He used the word "Strive." I looked up this verse in several translations. The KJV and NKJV both say, "Strive." The NIV says to "Make every effort." The NLT says, "Work hard" … to enter through the narrow gate, "for many…will seek to enter but will not be able." Jesus is speaking directly to His disciples, but He is also speaking to all of us. He is imploring us to strive, work hard, and to make every effort to enter the Kingdom. In Greek, the origin of the word 'strive' is 'agónizomai' which is derived from the root word 'agon.' According to Strong's Concordance, the definition of the word is as follows: I am struggling, striving [as in an athletic contest or warfare]; I contend, as with an adversary.

The people described in this verse thought they had faith. They even tell Jesus that they have shared food and drink with Him. Jesus taught in their streets. And sure, they probably went to church. Likely, these same people gave money to the less fortunate. But, on the day of judgment, there will be no more opportunity for redemption, and they will be dismayed, surprised, and pained when they realize that they had believed only a portion of the truth. They may have even gotten it almost right, but "almost right" will not save any soul. We can dismiss the opinions of men, but we cannot reject the infallible Word of God as the Spirit guides us in our understanding. You and I are singularly responsible for own souls. We must not allow ourselves to be misled; it's too important. We need to go to the Word of God, without bias or pre-conceived notions. We need to ask the Holy Spirit to teach us what is right. We should become students of His Word so that we are able to filter all that we hear through the Bible, as if it were a lie detector. Because, it is.

*"And **if you do not carry your own cross and follow me, you cannot be my disciple.** <u>But don't begin until you count the cost.</u> For who would begin construction of a building without first calculating the cost to **see if there is enough money to finish it?**"* {Luke 14:27-28 NLT}

Have you ever heard someone say, "It's just my cross to bear?" When Jesus lived on this earth, the cross wasn't necessarily a symbol of suffering, it was primarily a symbol of death. Jesus told them to put their own natural desires to death and forego their own plans for this life. He said to follow Him and do the will of the Father, every day. But, Jesus also said, don't bother starting to follow me unless you realize there is a cost, and we should be sure we are willing to go the entire distance so we'll make it to the finish line.

Placing trust in Christ is different than accepting facts and acknowledging that He lived, died and rose again. Jesus said that it's not what you say, but what you do, that He's interested in. Faith is something that you do. A believer is someone who trusts in the Lord. Obedience proves that you trust Him. *"But take heed to yourselves, lest your hearts be weighed down with carousing, drunkenness, and cares of this life, and that Day come on you unexpectedly. For it will come as a snare on all those who dwell on the face of the whole earth. Watch therefore, and <u>pray always that you may be counted worthy</u> to escape all these things that will come to pass, and to stand before the Son of Man."* {Luke 21:34-36}

What a perplexing verse. "Worthy to escape" is an honor bestowed on us. This is an appeal to be 'fitted' and 'prepared to stand.' We do this by staying in the process of sanctification as we remain in our on-going and active relationship with Christ. I believe that we are to approach the grace of God with a humble and teachable spirit. We should intently focus on learning and growing in our faith. If we are sincere about our relationship with Christ, we will not casually dismiss our willful sins.

He will strengthen us to the point that we can resist any adversary that would seek to lead us astray. However, all of us still have free will. If we choose the way of the world over the direction of God, then Christ will not force us into submission. He will, however, always be there for us, and He stands ready to hear our cries of repentance. When a prodigal son or daughter turns back from their own way and humbly returns to Him, the Lord always stands ready to intercede. Our heavenly father desires His children to submit to His will, not out of obligation, but out of love. He certainly did not create us to be robots, doing only what we're programmed to do. However, the Lord will relate to us on His terms, not ours.

During my period of "wandering," I remember hearing the voice of the enemy whisper to me. In my conscience, the enemy was saying things like: "What can you do for the Lord now?" "God won't use you anymore because you failed the test." He said, "You're not worthy." Lies. All lies. But, I struggled with the thoughts. I almost believed what I was hearing until I came to my senses and realized that I had to rely on God's Word, even if it didn't feel true at the moment. His Word promises that *"...God causes everything to work together for the good of those who love God and are called according to his purpose for them."* {Rom 8:28 NLT} This verse says that the Lord will cause EVERYTHING to work for our good, not just some things, but ALL things. This means He will use both the good and the bad. If we will just repent and turn our hearts towards home, the Lord will take our mess and turn it all around for our good and His glory.

*"I am the true vine, and my Father is the gardener. **He cuts off every branch <u>in me</u> that bears no fruit**, while every branch that does bear fruit he prunes so that it will be even more fruitful. You are already clean because of the word I have spoken to you. **Remain in me**, as I also remain in you. No branch can bear fruit by itself; it must remain in the vine. Neither can you bear fruit unless you remain in me. I am the vine; you are the branches. <u>**If you remain in me**</u> and I in you, you will bear much fruit; apart from me you can do nothing. <u>**If you do not remain in me**</u>, **you are like a branch that is thrown away and withers; such branches are picked up, thrown into the fire and burned.** If you remain in me and my words remain in you, ask whatever you wish, and it will be done for you. This is to*

*my Father's glory, that you bear much fruit, showing your-
selves to be my disciples."* {John 15:1-8 NIV}

So, let's take a closer look at this verse. Jesus was
speaking of every "person" that has faith in Him but is
not "bearing fruit." He specifically calls on us to "do
something" to produce fruit, and He tells us that if we
are to produce any fruit at all, we must abide in Him.
If we decide not to heed his warning and choose to go
our own way, then we will be cast out. In His exact
words, we will be picked up, thrown into the fire and
burned. Just to be clear, He is talking to believers.
These are not my words; these are the words of Jesus.
My point is that if we decide to rest comfortably in the
assurance that our eternity is entirely secure, even if we
are not "bearing fruit," we may be terribly mistaken.

So, for those of you who are counting on this
"eternal security," what do you do when you come to a
verse like this? Do you pause and ask the Lord to give
you a mind of wisdom and increase your understanding; or, do you just ignore it and make a conscious decision not to think about it? I contend that many
believers, and even well-intentioned pastors, do just
that.

*"You are My friends **if you do whatever I command
you.**"* {John 15:14} Now, I wonder why Jesus didn't say
it this way; you are my friends if you believe in me.
Instead, He added a qualifying word, "if" we do what
He commands.

*"For in it **the righteousness of God is revealed from
faith to faith;** as it is written, "The just shall live by faith.
For the wrath of God is revealed from heaven against all
ungodliness **and unrighteousness of men, who suppress
the truth** in unrighteousness, because what may be known*

of God is manifest in them, for God has shown it to them."
{Roman 1:17-19}

In other words, the wrath of God is against the people who suppress the truth by hiding or withholding the authentic teaching of the Word of God. Jesus explains that although people have obscured the truth, God will reveal it to the "just" through the Holy Spirit. Amen!! He is saying that because He is truly sovereign and in control He will reveal the true Word, by His Spirit and through His people. The truth will be revealed even if there are those who oppose, distort, hide it, or teach His Word in error. "It" is the truth that is being hidden by men. God is saying that He will not allow "it" to be suppressed entirely. He will make it manifest in the spirits of the "just." He will show it to them, so they are aware and not deceived.

*"... for all have sinned and fall short of the glory of God, being justified freely by His grace through the redemption that is in Christ Jesus, whom God set forth as a propitiation by His blood, through faith, to demonstrate His righteousness, because in His forbearance **God had passed over the sins that were previously committed**, to demonstrate at the present time His righteousness, that He might be just and **the justifier** of the one who has faith in Jesus. Where is boasting then? It is excluded. By what law? Of works? No, but by the law of faith. Therefore, we conclude that a man is **justified by faith** apart from the deeds of the law. Or is He the God of the Jews only? Is He not also the God of the Gentiles? Yes, of the Gentiles also, since there is one God who will justify the circumcised by faith and the uncircumcised through faith. **Do we then make void the law through faith? Certainly not! On the contrary, we establish the law."** {Romans 3:22-31}

When we repent, God passes over all prior sins. Don't overlook the last words of this verse. The law has

108

not become void as a result of our faith, it has been established. We actually have a higher calling than we did before. Why? Because we now have a knowledge of the truth. Our eyes and ears have been opened to discern right and wrong. We can receive correction from the Holy Spirit. We are expected to endure and to be steadfast to the end in our fellowship with Christ. He will enable us.

*"What shall we say then? **Shall we continue in sin that grace may abound? Certainly not! How shall we who died to sin live any longer in it?** Or do you not know that as many of us as were baptized into Christ Jesus were baptized into His death? Therefore, we were buried with Him through baptism into death, that just as Christ was raised from the dead by the glory of the Father, **even so, we also should walk in newness of life.**"* {Rom 6:1-4}

We need to stop sleep-walking through life and wake up spiritually. The alarm is going off, and it is sounding a "wake-up" call for endurance. Just as our physical body needs food, our spirit must also be nourished. If we stop eating for three days, what will happen to us? We'll lose energy, feel sick, and become easily tired. We won't be alert or prepared for the day. By the same token, when we eat healthy foods, our bodies naturally become stronger and more energetic. We'll become more resistant to disease and live longer. Similarly, spiritual food is what our souls require in order to grow in our knowledge of Christ. The Bible provides us with sustenance for our souls, and the study of the Bible is critical for our eternal well-being.

When the Bible becomes our filter, it will guide us down a path of righteousness and peace. And just to clarify, peace is not the absence of problems in our life. To be at peace is to be calm in your heart, regardless of what is going on around you.

*"But people who aren't spiritual can't receive these truths from God's Spirit. It all sounds foolish to them and they can't understand it, **for only those who are spiritual can understand what the Spirit means.**"* {1 Cor 2:14 NLT}

*"Do you not know that **you are the temple of God** and that the Spirit of God dwells in you? If anyone defiles the temple of God, God will destroy him. For the temple of God is holy, which temple you are."* {1 Cor 3:16-17} Unbelievers are not the temple of God. The Bible refers to unbelievers as "sons of Satan," until they come to repentance and receive grace through Christ. Therefore, we can reasonably conclude that this verse was written to believers.

*"Do you not know that in a race all the runners run, but only one gets the prize? **Run in such a way as to get the prize. Everyone who competes in the games goes into strict training.** They do it to get a crown that will not last, but **we do it to get a crown that will last forever.** Therefore, I do not run like someone running aimlessly; I do not fight like a boxer beating the air. No, I strike a blow to my body and make it my slave **so that after I have preached to others, I myself will not be disqualified for the prize.**"* {1 Cor 9:24-27}

I hired a personal trainer named Joe. I am one of those people that needs accountability to help me stay committed to the process, so I enlisted Joe as my coach. I'm sharing an awful lot of information, but I wanted to lose 10-15 pounds. To get the results that I want and to ensure they last, I've had to change my lifestyle and re-program my eating habits. My workouts primarily consist of weightlifting, and Joe pushes me hard. He explained that I must tell my body what it's going to do. Why? Because my body doesn't want to change. So, to produce a change, I have to discipline my body. I submit to workouts that make me uncomfortable, and sometimes they even hurt a little, but Joe continually reminds me that the results will be worth it.

Paul says that he forces his body into subjection to his spirit rather than allowing his natural desires to win over. If he did not do this, then he states that even he, the great Apostle Paul, could become disqualified. If there were anyone in Scripture that seems to have a guaranteed assurance of salvation, it would surely be the Apostle Paul. Instead, by his example, he encourages us to remain humble, to be self-aware and to walk daily in close fellowship with Christ. We are instructed to lead our lives through discipline and to run our race in a way that we will obtain the prize. This goes along with what Jesus said when He told us to first count the cost before we even start to follow Him. I've read commentary that asserts Paul was not saying he could lose his salvation, but rather, that he could lose the privilege of sharing the gospel with others. Nonsense. What a great example of twisting Scripture to say what one wants them to say.

'Adokimos' is the Greek word used for disqualified. It means failing to pass the test, or unapproved and counterfeit. Unfortunately, the Bible can be twisted by people with good intentions who feel a sense of obligation to explain away verses that blatantly contradict the teaching of eternal security.

This can be difficult information to process.

When we choose to live in sin after we have received grace, we might try to rationalize with ourselves, so we can continue down our own path without feeling overwhelmed by the truth of God's Word. We could find ourselves thinking or saying that God loves me, and He knows my heart. Yes, He does, and Yes, He does. He loves us, and that is why He gave us His Word, to

111

protect us from ourselves. The worst thing we can ever do is lie to ourselves. If we blatantly choose to sin, then we should at least call a spade a spade, but we should never attempt to twist God's Word so that we can feel better about our choices. We need to have our eyes wide open, so we will not be deceived. If we ignore the convictions of the Holy Spirit and lie to ourselves about God's Word, we will become spiritually blind.

I would love to be able to embrace the "Once Saved, Always Saved" concept. I want to be confident in the fact that I am eternally secure, no matter what I do or don't do. But, I think we would be wise to consider the practice of the Bereans in Thessalonica and find out for ourselves what the Scriptures say. One of my best girlfriends, Teresa Gardner, shared a precious truth with me. She said, "We are all just walking each other home." It is so important to check in frequently and intentionally with our friends, family, and other believers to encourage one another to stay the course.

In the same way that I hired a trainer to hold me accountable in my pursuit of a higher level of physical health, my Christian friends are an invaluable source of accountability and meaningful encouragement. If you don't have these types of friends, ask the Lord to send Godly people into your life. We become like those we hang around.

*"Let us not become weary in doing good, for at the proper time we will reap a harvest **if we do not give up**. Therefore, as we have opportunity, let us do good to all people, especially to those who belong to the family of believers."* {Gal 6:9-10 NIV}

There it is again, that conditional word, "if."

*"For I have told you often before, and I say it again with tears in my eyes, that there are **many** whose conduct shows **they are really enemies of the cross** of Christ. **They are headed for destruction.** Their god is their appetite, they brag about shameful things, and **they think only about this life here on earth.**"* {Phil 3:18-19 NLT}

I believe that Paul is referring to the many who profess to be Christians. He is speaking of those who think they know God but don't actually pursue a true relationship with Him. These people genuinely believe they have eternal life. Paul is heartbroken and weeping because they don't understand that in reality they are enemies of the cross. These people have set their minds on their own plans and pursuits, and they don't follow Christ with endurance.

Is it any different today?

Every weekend, the pews are full of people who sing the songs and profess faith on Sunday, but whose daily lives bear little to no resemblance of one who has the indwelling of the Holy Spirit. According to Paul, it is entirely possible to sit in that pew every Sunday, and still be an enemy of the cross. *"And you, who once were alienated and enemies in your mind by wicked works, yet now He has reconciled in the body of His flesh through death, to present you holy, and blameless, and above reproach in His sight--**if indeed you continue in the faith, grounded and steadfast, and are not moved away from the hope of the gospel which you heard,** which was preached to every creature under heaven, of which I, Paul, became a minister."* {Col 1:21-23}

Once again, "if." These are conditions! If grace was enough, why would Paul say this? Paul even said that to be counted above reproach by God, we must not be moved away from the hope of the gospel. Is that possible? These are stern warnings, and I believe that we would all be wise to heed them. *"So then, just as you received Christ Jesus as Lord,* **continue to live your lives in him, rooted and built up in him, strengthened in the faith as you were taught,** *and overflowing with thankfulness."* {2 Col 2:6-7 NIV}

"Now the Holy Spirit tells us clearly that **in the last times some will turn away from the true faith;** *they will follow deceptive spirits and teachings that come from demons."* {1 Timothy 4:1 NLT} *The NIV says, some will abandon the faith, and the NKJV says some shall depart from the faith.*

If one could count on the power of grace to hold him or her eternally secure, regardless of their own future decisions, then what does Paul mean when he said that there will be some who will "depart from the faith?" Paul warned of apostasy: "Giving heed to seducing spirits" is one way to fall from grace. The love of money is another way. Paul warned: *"For the love of money is a root of all kinds of evil.* **Some people, eager for money, have wandered from the faith** *and pierced themselves with many griefs."* {1 Tim 6:10 NIV}

" since it is a righteous thing with God to repay with tribulation those who trouble you, and to give you who are troubled rest with us when the Lord Jesus is revealed from heaven with His mighty angels, in flaming fire **taking vengeance on those who do not know God,** <u>**and**</u> **on** <u>**those who do not obey**</u> **the gospel of our Lord Jesus Christ. These shall be punished with everlasting destruction** *from the presence of the Lord and from the glory of His power,"* {2 Thes 1:7-9}

Wake Up! Warning. Red Flag. This verse covers two categories of people upon whom vengeance will fall:

114

1) Those who do not know God – Unbelievers

2) And, those who do not obey the gospel of our Lord Jesus Christ. Believers and Unbelievers.

Mighty angels? Flaming fire? Vengeance? Even for some of the people in the pew on Sunday? I said earlier that the Bible doesn't necessarily market well, and this is a great example. There are many Christians who adamantly refuse to believe everything that the Bible says. As a society, we often reject things that make us uncomfortable. In the same vein, we have really been conditioned to think of God only as graceful and forgiving, not jealous and vengeful. However, if we skip these parts of the Bible it's like fast forwarding through the scary parts of a movie. When you fast forward, you didn't really see the movie, and you'll likely be confused about what happens in the end. Don't skip this point...notice that the believers who disobey the gospel are grouped with the unbelievers as the recipients of the Lord's final vengeance. Paul says that all of them will be punished with everlasting destruction. Hell. It's a real place. Don't be misled or even confused about what happens in the End.

*"and also, if anyone competes in athletics, **<u>he is not crowned unless</u>** he competes <u>according to the rules</u>. The hard-working farmer must be first to partake of the crops. **Consider what I say, and may the Lord give you understanding in all things.**"* {2 Tim 2:5-7} The writer is pleading for us to read between the lines. He says, "consider what I say," and he hopes the Lord will give us the understanding to comprehend what he is telling us. "He is not crowned **unless** he competes according to the rules." If we hope for a prize, we must not only run the race, we must also submit ourselves to the terms and conditions of the race.

*"You should know this, Timothy, that **in the last days there will be very difficult times.** For people will love only themselves and their money. They will be boastful and proud, scoffing at God, disobedient to their parents, and ungrateful. They will consider nothing sacred. They will be unloving and unforgiving; they will slander others and have no self-control. **They will be** cruel and hate what is good. They will betray their friends, be reckless, be puffed up with pride, and **love pleasure rather than God. They will act religious, but they will reject the power that could make them godly. Stay away from people like that!** ...forever following new teachings, but they are never able to understand the truth...They have depraved minds and a counterfeit faith.** But they won't get away with this for long. Someday everyone will recognize what fools they are...* {2 Tim 3:1-5; 7-9 NLT}

I don't know about you, but this sounds like a very familiar and fitting description of our societies and culture today. Do you realize that we can squelch the Holy Spirit by our unbelief? If you want to be open to the power of God operating in your life, but you struggle with your belief, then pray. Ask the Lord to help you with your unbelief. He does not change. He is the same God throughout all generations. He still operates in the same ways.

*"This is a faithful saying and these things I want you to affirm <u>constantly</u>, that **those who have believed in God should be careful to maintain good works.** These things are good and profitable to men."* {Titus 3:8}

*"For **it is impossible** for **those who were once enlightened,** and **have tasted the heavenly gift, and have become partakers of the Holy Spirit, and have tasted the good word of God** and the powers of the age to come, **"if they fall away, to renew them again to repentance,** since they crucify again for themselves the Son of God, and*

*put Him to an open shame. For the earth which drinks in the rain that often comes upon it and bears herbs useful for those by whom it is cultivated, receives blessing from God; **but if it bears thorns and briars, it is rejected and near to being cursed, whose end is to be burned.***" {Heb 6:4-8}

Admittedly, this was a difficult verse for me. I have experienced a season of wandering from God and I had to ask God to help me understand what this verse truly means. The Holy Spirit has shown me that "wandering" and "falling away" are different. Paul talks of those that wander, and he says that whomever turns the wanderer back, helps save their soul from death. We find an example of wandering through the parable of the prodigal son and the story of Peter denying that he knew Christ because he feared the reaction of the people. But, falling away completely is another matter. Falling away is total apostasy. Apostasy is described as the abandonment and renunciation of one's faith or religious beliefs. As followers of Christ, we may fall frequently, but I believe there is a clear distinction between falling and falling away altogether. If we are abiding in Christ, we are never in jeopardy of apostasy. Apostasy, or "falling away," always begins in the mind.

One can be seduced by doctrines that sound right but are not rooted in biblical truth. People can be more committed to the Church and the activities of religion, than they are to the Word of God. The entire book of Hebrews is like no other in the New Testament. In Hebrews, we learn how Christ purified us from our sins through His perfect sacrifice. We learn that He has become our High Priest and that we no longer need a man to intercede for us. We learn that Jesus is our shepherd and that He will never leave or forsake us.

The book of Hebrews is also persistent in its warnings about the danger of living a casual and careless Christian life. But, the warnings are not about losing heavenly rewards. Instead, they warn us of the peril of our souls and the possibility of spending eternity outside the presence of God.

I have read many views and numerous opinions on this passage. Some have interpreted the Scripture as referring to those who were enlightened but who only had an intellectual knowledge of God. Another view suggests that the people being described are actually unbelievers who may have tasted the heavenly gift, but only for a moment. They may have expressed faith, but they did not exercise a genuine, saving faith. I submit to you that I believe both of these positions to be in error. The Scripture says, "they have become partakers of the Holy Spirit." We know this to be a sign and seal of genuine faith. The Holy Spirit will never leave or forsake us. This makes perfect sense if you consider something I mentioned earlier. Our seal is a "deposit" awaiting an inheritance, if and only if, we endure. I liken this to a child being written into a parent's will. Once written in, the child expects an inheritance, and while it is unlikely a parent will ever stop loving their child, it is entirely possible for the parent, to write the child out of a will at a later time.

If we are faced with God's Word but hold to our position and pride, rather than repent when our guilty conscience is convicted of sin, it can lead to a seared conscience. *"Such teachings come through hypocritical liars, whose consciences have been seared as with a hot iron."* {1 Tim 4:2} If we violate our conscience and do not repent, we will eventually become hardened. We can reach a point when our conscience is no longer sensitive to sin. In this state, a person is capable of willfully and habitually committing sins without even realizing it. Why? Because once the conscience has been seared, there is no longer any conviction from the Holy Spirit. {1 Thes 5:16; Heb 3:13}

In Greek, the word seared means 'cauterized' which results in the destruction of our spiritual nerve endings. Paul explains where apostasy leads, and he urgently implores us not to ignore our call to righteous living. When we are firmly rooted in Christ and in an active relationship with our King, we will recognize and discern the voice of the shepherd. We will not be led away by a counterfeit. In 1 Corinthians chapter 2, we are taught that it is only the Spirit of God that knows the mind of God, and it is only the Spirit that can give us understanding. There are many theologians, liberal Christian professors and students of the Bible that do not seek the Spirit of God for wisdom and knowledge as they read and study Scripture. They are simply pursuing academic learning. As a result, they are getting it wrong, and worse still, they are teaching it wrong.

As a true believer, *"you have been set free from sin and have become slaves to righteousness."* {Rom 6:18}

If we continue to sin with no concern or sorrow and then we expect grace without a heart that is broken and repentant, we have insulted the Spirit of grace. To speak of God's judgment is not pleasant, and it is not a welcomed conversation for most people. Many people and many churches had rather just avoid it. I understand. It hurts people's feelings. And, it makes a lot of churchgoers, both new and old, feel uncomfortable. However, it is necessary to understand that salvation does not come to those who only believe in God.

Unless you are sincerely calling on the Lord in your last dying breaths, a profession of faith has no value if it stands alone. The bottom line is that saving

119

faith is trusting in Christ as Lord, and it is not separate from His Lordship. If He is Lord, then He is your Master. Jesus said, *"Why do you call me, Lord, Lord, and do not do what I say?"* {Luke 6:46}

The "many" traveling on the broad road will include religious people. According to the Bible, these people have a form of Godliness. They look and act the part, but they are deceived. What lulls people into this deception? Could it be a superficial understanding of the gospel? The Lord wants our obedience. He wants our inner-self. He wants our heart. A true believer will be consumed with love for Christ. An authentic and committed believer will have a thirst for God's Word. Obedience will flow from the heart, and obedience is key. *"If you love Me, keep My commandments."* {John 14:15}

Do you know why we have been given grace?

*"Through Him **we have received grace** and apostleship **for obedience to the faith** among all nations for His name."* {Rom 1:5}

CHAPTER SEVEN

Brief History of Christianity, Doctrine, and Covenants

Men may interpret the Bible, but men are not above it. It may surprise you to know that the popular "Once Saved Always Saved" doctrine is actually a relatively new phenomenon within the Christian faith. In fact, the doctrine remained virtually untaught until the 16th century.

This begs the obvious question...Why?

To better understand the Scriptures, we need to understand the history of our faith and especially our church doctrine. Christianity began as an ethnically Jewish religion. It had many stages of development, starting with the Old Covenant between God and the Israelites. This Covenant was named after Moses and was known as the 'Mosaic Covenant.' It was characterized by a commitment to the written Scriptures called "the law." The "law" had several tenants, the most important of which were the intentional separation of Jews from non-Jews and dietary restrictions. The Jews believed that there was only one God, and this belief was, of course, not compatible with the worship of the Roman emperor.

In the early Christian period, there were three religious' sects of Jews. They were called the Pharisees, the Sadducees, and the Essenes. Each of them claimed to represent true Judaism. The Sadducees and Pharisees were priests, but they had different interpretations of the Mosaic Law. The Sadducees are best characterized as the ruling and priestly class of Jerusalem. They were fully devoted to the temple and insisted on the literal interpretation of Scripture which consisted of the first five books of the Old Testament. The first five books are called the Torah. The Pharisees were theological teachers. In addition to the Torah, however, they also honored laws that had been passed down by oral tradition.

Unlike the Sadducees, the Pharisees believed in a bodily resurrection. The Essene were characterized by extreme self-discipline. They also carefully followed ceremonial rituals regarding purity, and they adhered to a doctrine that was likely to be understood by only a small number of people with specialized knowledge. It is believed that the Essene produced the Dead Sea Scrolls. Lastly, a political group formed. Its members were called the Zealots, and they passionately sought political liberation from Rome. Each of these groups had their own interests and teachings.

After the death, resurrection, and ascension of Jesus, the primitive Church was a community led by Jesus' apostles and His relatives. In the book of Acts, we can find information about Pentecost, the establishment of the Jerusalem Church and the spread of the faith among the Gentiles. We also find the details of Paul's conversion and of his imprisonment in Rome during the mid-first century.

Before his conversion to Christianity, Paul was known by the name of Saul. Saul had been vigorously opposed to Christianity and he had been known to persecute and imprison Christians. Despite his fierce opposition, Paul had a dramatic experience which we know as the *Damascus Road conversion* in which he was temporarily blinded and then he was confronted by Jesus. Afterward, he received the Holy Spirit, and immediately began preaching the Christian gospel. Paul's teaching was centered on helping the Church understand the death and resurrection of Jesus Christ as the New Covenant, and with it, the end of the requirement to live under the Jewish requirements of the Old Covenant. Paul also began to teach the power of God indwelling believers through the Holy Spirit. He proclaimed that the Gentiles had the same access to faith and freedom from the law as the Jews.

At the time, Paul taught from the Old Testament, which was all the Scripture he had. Little did he know that he and the disciples were actually writing the New Testament. The earliest texts were the Epistles written between 50-62 AD. These were written by Paul to various Christian communities.

The earliest known completed version of the New Testament didn't begin circulating until the late 4th century. Conflict quickly began. The fact that rights had been bestowed on Gentile (non-Jewish) believers was blasphemous to some of the Jews. Many argued that before a Gentile could become a Christian, they would have to "become Jewish."

At the time, "becoming Jewish" usually referred to the need to be circumcised, as well as the adherence to the strict dietary law. The doctrines of the apostles brought the Early Church into even deeper conflict.

123

The earliest controversies were generally related to the person of Jesus. Was He eternally divine or human? The primary questions centered on how Jesus could be both Savior and God. After all, wasn't Jesus the son of Joseph the carpenter? In the first Century, Christianity began to spread from Jerusalem throughout the Roman Empire. It grew primarily as a Jewish sect. In the early 4th century, a Roman soldier named Constantine won a significant victory in battle and was crowned the Emperor of Rome. Constantine had been exposed to Christianity by his mother, Helena, and he publicly attributed his military success to the Christian God. As a result, Christianity became the official religion of the Roman Empire. Named for the emperor Constantine, the city of Constantinople was officially founded in 324 AD on the site of the already existing city of Byzantium. It was the capital city of the Roman empire and one of Europe's largest and wealthiest cities. It also served as the center of the Christian Church. Interestingly, Constantinople fell to the Ottomans in 1453 and today it is the modern-day city of Istanbul, Turkey. Soon after he became Emperor, Constantine organized a council whose job it was to establish precisely what the Christian faith was, and then to determine what it would become. In 325 AD, the First Council of Nicea arranged the laws and rules into an order or a codified system.

Over the next few centuries, controversies and debates over the precise interpretation of the faith were prevalent. The many differences in Christian practices and beliefs increased when Rome fell in 476. Suddenly, Eastern and Western Christians were no longer under the same political rule. When the Eastern and Western divisions of the Church did not resolve, the Church split.

This created two churches, the Greek Orthodox and the Roman Catholic church. From the beginning and throughout the ages, Christians were subject to persecution, but it has always been the Jews who have suffered mercilessly. Unknown to many modern-day believers, much of the Jewish persecution was due to the encouragement or the willful ignorance of Church leaders. Some of these early Church leaders developed a warped view of the Jewish people and essentially charged them all, in the court of public opinion, with the death of Jesus Christ. This had a significant impact on feelings for the Jewish people and has fueled anti-Semitism through the centuries.

John Chrysostom (349-407) was the Archbishop of Constantinople, and he is revered as a saint and a renowned theologian. However, he also penned some writings on the Jewish people that were said to be "the most horrible and violent denunciations of Judaism to be found in the writings of any Christian theologian." He had described them as "lustful, rapacious, greedy, perfidious bandits, inveterate murderers, men possessed by the devil." Oddly enough, he even said, "I hate the synagogue precisely because it has the law and the prophets... I hate the Jews also because they outrage the law..."

Then came the Crusades (1095-1291), which are an integral part of the history of anti-Semitism in the Middle Ages. We think of the Crusades as an attempt to re-capture the Holy Land from the Muslim rule; but, during the Crusades, entire Jewish communities were massacred. Even while carrying the cross as a sacred emblem and after capturing Jerusalem, the Crusaders raped, plundered and murdered the Jewish people on their way back through Europe.

In the 15th and 16th centuries came the Spanish Inquisitions. During this time, Spain was a dominant power in Europe and wielded considerable influence in the region.

King Ferdinand and Queen Isabella made an official request to the Roman Catholic Church asking them to investigate Jews who they believed had falsely converted to Christianity. Jews were given four months to convert to Christianity or leave the country. Based on the decree, if a Jew did not leave Spain or convert by the deadline of July 31, 1492, then they were brutally tortured and burned at the stake.

The groundwork for the basis of Protestantism was laid by the Reformation of the early 16th-century Church. Martin Luther and Huldrych Zwingli were two Theologians who set out to intentionally reform the Church between 1521-1579. History notes that they perceived the corruption within the Church to be a perversion of the doctrine itself. As a result, the main objective of the Reformation was to alter contemporary doctrines giving prominence to what they deemed to be the "true gospel." The leaders of the Reformation called themselves "evangelical emphasizing a return to the true gospel."

Martin Luther was a German professor of theology. Luther was also a priest and published his influential *Ninety-Five These of 1517*. He had expected that the Jews would be convinced by his logic and that they would convert to Christianity. But, when they did not convert, Luther was upset and turned on the Jewish people altogether. He wrote another 60,000-word dissertation entitled, *The Jews and Their Lies* (1543). In it, he reasoned that the Jews were no longer God's Chosen People and referred to them as "the devil's people." He advocated setting their synagogues on fire, forbidding rabbis from preaching, seizing Jewish property, taking money and smashing up their homes, so these "envenomed worms" would be forced into labor or expelled "for all time."

The first time I read this, I was in shock. I mean, come on... really? Martin Luther was one of the most influential leaders of the Christian faith. However, historians assert that Luther's anti-Jewish rhetoric significantly contributed to the development of anti-Semitism in Germany. Church Historian Martin Brecht had this to say of Luther, "There was a world of difference between his (Luther's) belief in salvation and his racial ideology. Nevertheless, his misguided agitation had an evil result. Luther fatefully became one of the 'Church fathers' of anti-Semitism and thus provided material for the universal hatred of the Jews, cloaking it with the authority of the reformer."

Another leader of the Reformation era was John Calvin. Calvin was a lawyer who fled France after his conversion to the Protestant cause. It is important to note that Calvin strongly agreed with Luther's' teaching on justification by faith, and he also stressed the doctrine of predestination.

Revivalism transpired between 1720 and 1906. This period was also referred to as the Calvinist and Wesleyan revival. In North America, it was called the Great Awakening. This era marked the beginning of the evangelical Protestants. During this time, the Presbyterian, Baptist, and new Methodist churches were formed. From 1730-1740, there was a spiritual renewal that swept through the American Colonies, infusing them with religious enthusiasm. Until this movement, Christians had generally become complacent, but the Great Awakening put an emphasis on Godly preaching and encouraged a deep sense of true repentance and sanctification through Christ.

The final group to emerge from the "great awakenings" in North America were the Pentecosts. Pentecostalism started in the era of 1906 and had its roots in the Methodist, Wesleyan, and Holiness movements. It would later lead to the Charismatic movement. The history of the Church in contemporary times covers the period from the revolutions of 1848 to today.

Following the early years of the Reformation, the doctrine of "assurance" became a growing issue. Some purport that the entire Protestant Reformation was an issue over the questions of assurance. How could a Christian find balance between the certainty of their salvation and the clear message of persevering and living in the Spirit rather than the flesh? Luther had separated the law and the Gospel into different theological corners. However, everyone did not agree. In turn, this led to the introduction of Antinomianism, which is the certainty of God's promises without the observance of His commands. Antinomianism teaches that the believer is entirely free from all obligation to the law. According to this philosophy, the concession to legal duty was an infringement upon free grace.

Merriam-Webster defines Antinomian as:

1) One who holds that under the gospel dispensation of grace, the moral law is of no use or obligation because faith alone is necessary for salvation.

2) One who rejects a socially established morality.

In short, once the Reformation principle of justification by faith alone took shape, Protestant churches faced a new temptation to drop the need for works altogether.

This cleared the path for Christians to freely indulge in immoral and worldly behavior since works, allegedly, had no bearing on one's salvation. As a result, pastors were now forced to balance the comfort of assurance with the divine mandate to finish the spiritual race set before the Church.

According to Luther, "The first understanding and use of the Law is to restrain the wicked. This civil restraint is extremely necessary and was instituted by God." The second use is evangelical, driving sinners away from their own righteousness to trust in Christ alone. The Puritans were a group of English Protestants of the late 16th and 17th centuries who considered the reformation of the Church of England as incomplete. They had a third use of the law. The Puritans viewed the law as a directive, meaning they looked to the law as a "rule of life" that would guide them in ways that were pleasing to God, so they dedicated themselves to living life according to God's will.

Calvin's teachings had one very significant difference: assurance. The final tenet of Calvinism is *Perseverance of the Saints*, which is known today by many names, including the "once saved always saved doctrine," "the impossibility of apostasy," "the security of the believer" and "once in grace, always in grace." Before the time of John Calvin, there had been no public claims that it was impossible for a true Christian to lose his or her salvation. This "once saved, always saved" theology was not even shared by Martin Luther and his followers. This doctrine was introduced in the mid-sixteenth century, and it was a teaching that would likely have been condemned as a dangerous heresy by the previous generations of Christians.

This teaching would have been inconceivable to predestination believers, such as Augustine. Just two years before he died, in his book called *The Gift of Perseverance*, he taught the concept that not everyone who was predestined to come to God's grace was actually predestined to remain with him until glory. In fact, this was the teaching of Augustine, Fulgentius, Aquinas, and even Luther until the time of Calvin. As it relates to the anti-Semitism within the Church and the mistreatment of the Jewish people throughout the centuries, here is what the Lord has to say about that. *"But I am very angry with the other nations that are now enjoying peace and security. I was only a little angry with my people [Israel], but the nations inflicted harm on them [Israel] far beyond my intentions."* {Zech 1:15 NLT}

It's sort of like a father who is in the front yard and sees his son being disobedient, so he bends him over his knee and gives him a swat on the bottom to discipline him. After the Father returns to the house, the neighbor who had been watching from the window goes into the father's yard and begins to beat the son with a lead pipe. With good reason, the father is now furious with the neighbor and would likely respond with wrath. Yes, God had been just a "little angry" with Israel, but it was not the responsibility of other nations or even the Church leaders to harm His chosen people. God is well aware of the travails of His beloved people, and He speaks of them often. But, nowhere in the Bible does Israel lose its status as the apple of God's eye. In fact, the opposite occurs. He remains committed to the restoration of their land and promises that those who bring harm to Israel will be dealt with severely.

He warns, *"For this is what the LORD Almighty says: "After the Glorious One has sent me against the nations that have plundered you—for whoever touches you [Israel] touches the apple of his eye—I will surely raise my hand against them so that their slaves will plunder them. Then you will know that the LORD Almighty has sent me."* {Zech 2:8-9 -NIV}

History proves that Scripture is powerful and active, but we've also seen that the perversion and the misrepresentation of God's Word can have disastrous consequences. It can be used as the basis to eradicate an entire people, and it can even threaten our eternal security "if" we choose to disregard it. So, the stage has been set. Now that we've reviewed a bit of our Church history, let's take a look at the Old and New Covenants. We will examine the difference between the law and the covenants. Then, perhaps we can understand what has changed and what has not.

Old and New Testament Covenants

Everything written in the Old Testament, especially what happened to Israel, was written to teach us God's character and to instruct us on what He wants from His people. The travails of the Israelites are a great example of what can happen when we turn away from Him, but the Old Testament also shows us the depth of God's love for His people. It is through the Old Testament that we confirm Jesus as the fulfillment of prophecy, the promised Messiah. Finally, the New Testament prepares us for what we should expect in the last days.

"For everything that was written in the past was written to teach us, so that through the endurance taught in the Scriptures and the encouragement they provide we might have hope." {Rom15:4}

All of Christ's apostles followed His example. The apostle John wrote: *"Now by this, **we know that we know Him if we keep His commandments.** He who says, 'I know Him,' and does not keep His commandments, is a liar, and the truth is not in him"* {1 John 2:3-4}.

Similarly, Paul taught that **"keeping the commandments of God is what matters"** {1 Corinthians 7:19}. Though it may be surprising to some, the New Testament carries with it an even higher standard than the Old. In the New Covenant, we are given the power through Christ to actually obey God's commands. This means that we will be held to a higher standard, and according to Scripture, that our punishment will be even more severe than the people in the Old Testament if we turn away from righteousness.

When Paul was ministering to the early Church, the New Testament did not yet exist. So, when did the Old Testament begin to no longer apply? Many leaders within the Church, generally regard the apostle Paul as having paved the way for modern-day Christianity.

It is assumed that Paul helped transition Christianity from its uniquely Jewish roots and positioned the New Covenant as a replacement for the centuries-old biblical law. But is that what actually happened? Let's not be confused. When we review the Old and New Testaments collectively, we see the fullness of God's love, as well as the lengths He has gone to prove His love for us. We also see prophecy that reveals the fullness of God's plans for the end of the ages. When we focus on one without the other, we risk misunderstanding much of the intended message and meaning. As Christians, we must learn from "all Scripture." This is especially true as it relates to understanding and abiding by the teachings of the New Covenant. None of the Old Testament Scriptures are irrelevant! *"All Scripture is given by inspiration of God, and is profitable for doctrine, for reproof, for correction, for instruction in righteousness, that the man of God may be complete, thoroughly equipped for every good work."* {2 Tim 3:16-17}

If we look closely at the words and actions of Jesus, He never contradicts the instructions that God gave to Moses or the prophets. Jesus plainly tells us that He did not intend to destroy anything in the law. Jesus explained that He was the key that would unlock everything. He was teaching us how to apply God's instructions to mankind on a personal level. The Lord is concerned with who we are on the inside, our most authentic selves, rather than who we are presenting ourselves to be on the outside. He said," *You clean the outside of the cup and dish, but inside they are full of greed and self-indulgence...First, clean the inside of the cup and dish, and then the outside also will be clean."* {Matt 23:26-27}

"Do not think that I came to destroy the Law *or the Prophets. I did not come to destroy but to fulfill.* **"***For assuredly, I say to you,* **till heaven and earth pass away, one jot or one tittle will by no means pass from the law till all is fulfilled."** {Matt 5:17-18}

Jesus' sacrificial death eliminated the requirement for animal sacrifices and ritualistic ceremonies. These ceremonies had foreshadowed His death in our place. {Hebrews 10:1-10} When Jesus spoke in Matthew 5:17, He knew His sacrifice would be twisted out of context, implying the entire body of the Old Testament law was no longer necessary. Many Christians have believed, and still believe to this day, that they are no longer under the law and instead are covered by grace. So, because of grace, they assert that there is no longer a need to pursue righteousness or even a requirement to abide by the Lord's commands. This is a lie. Do not be deceived!

The Old Covenant is a description of the agreement God made with Moses to take care of His people if they followed His ways. The Mosaic law consisted of three parts:

1) the *Ten Commandments*,

2) the *ordinances*, and

3) the *worship system,* which included the priesthood, the tabernacle, the offerings and the festivals.

{Exodus 20-40; Lev 1-7;23}
The law was intended to describe His ways.

As time passed, God's people (the Israelites), began to misinterpret or disregard the agreements of the Covenant. They failed to keep the requirements of the Old Covenant for the remission of their sins. They lost their reverence for God, and they even sacrificed blind or lame animals on the altar of God. By continuing these sacrilegious practices, they faced the danger of being condemned and executed by order of the law. Jesus was crucified as a sin offering for us, and He fulfilled the law by becoming the innocent sacrificial lamb, without blemish. He was without sin, and yet He became sin. He took the penalty for our sins by the shedding of His blood, once and for all. This meant that the daily sacrifices of the Old Covenant were no longer required. There are also some symbolic aspects of the Old Covenant which are no longer required. These symbolic aspects are clearly defined in the book of Hebrews. They are *"concerned only with foods and drinks, various washings, and fleshly ordinances imposed until the time of reformation."* {Hebrews 9:10}.

More than 500 years before Jesus was born, the promise of the New Covenant was given by God through the prophet Jeremiah. *"But this is the covenant that I will make with the house of Israel after those days, says the Lord: **I will put My law in their minds, and write it on their hearts;** and I will be their God, and they shall be My people"* {Jer 31:33}

The promise was never intended to lower the standards for defining righteousness! It was given to change the location of where the existing laws of right-eousness would be written by writing them into our hearts. The promise was about refining the character of God's people through their hearts, so we would be capable and equipped to become the people of God.

*"For if that first covenant had been faultless, then no place would have been sought for a second. Because **finding fault with them**, He says: 'Behold, the days are coming, says the Lord, when I will make a new covenant with the house of Israel and with the house of Judah ...'"* {Hebrews 8:7-8}

God found fault with the people. The weakness in the agreement was not in the law itself. God had given the people His righteous laws, but they had not yet received a righteous heart. The promise God gave the Israelites through the New Covenant was that, at a future time, He would change their hearts. Then, they would have a sincere desire to please Him, and He would enable them to obey the laws by the power from the Holy Spirit.

The prophet Ezekiel foretold how this promise would be fulfilled: *"I will give you a new heart and put a new spirit within you; I will take the heart of stone out of your flesh and give you a heart of flesh. **I will put My Spirit within you and cause you to walk in My statutes, and you will keep My judgments and do them.**"* {Ezekiel 36:26}

Jesus was asked, *"Good Teacher, what good thing shall I do that I may have eternal life?"* Jesus answered him directly: ***"If you want to enter into life, keep the commandments"*** {Matthew 19:16-17}.

The laws remain valid, but the way in which we obey them was transformed by the death, resurrection, and the ascension of Jesus Christ.

After Jesus had risen, He was walking along a road and met two of the disciples, but they did not recognize Him. The disciples were talking with each other about the prophet that had been handed over to death. They were puzzled because they heard his tomb was now empty. *"He said to them, "How foolish you are, and how slow to believe all that the prophets have spoken! Did not the Messiah have to suffer these things and then enter his glory? And beginning with Moses and all the Prophets, he explained to them what was said in all the Scriptures concerning himself."* {Luke 24:25-27}

The fulfillment of the prophecies contained in the Old Testament establish Jesus as the Messiah. Jesus pointed this out to them because their faith had to be based on Moses, the prophets, and on all of the Scriptures. They needed to understand this clearly, so they would be able to proclaim the gospel and to effectively present Jesus as the fulfillment of the Messianic prophecies. Jesus also said to them, *"This is what I told you while I was still with you: Everything must be fulfilled that is written about me in the Law of Moses, the Prophets, and the Psalms. Then he opened their minds so they could understand the Scriptures."* {Luke 24:44-45}

If the law is obsolete and void, then by what standard is righteousness measured? Absent the law there is no way we would know what sin is. *"...by the law comes the knowledge of sin."* {Rom 3:20}

When we removed God from our schools (and generally from our society as a whole), we removed the moral compass for determining right and wrong. The sad reality is that the children in this era are growing up in a generation of confusion and spiritual darkness. Let's consider what Paul said...

"What shall we say then? Is the law sin? Certainly not! On the contrary, I would not have known sin except through the law. For I would not have known covetousness unless the law had said, "You shall not covet." {Rom 7:7}

The Old Covenant was given out of the law, but the Old Covenant and the law are not one in the same. When He gave the Old Covenant, the Lord was giving a promise of protection and blessing out of love, mercy, and grace. However, the Old Covenant also contained a clear expectation of judgment and death to those who broke it. God did not intend to destroy His law by removing the Old Covenant. The covenant, whether old or new, was and is the means of fulfilling the law. Providing a means to fulfill the law was God's way of establishing it.

We have been given the Holy Spirit to lead us in all wisdom and to teach us *"that the righteous requirement of the law might be fulfilled in us who do not walk according to the flesh but according to the Spirit."* {Rom. 8:4}

"Blessed is the man who does not walk in the counsel of the wicked or stand in the way of sinners or sit in the seat of mockers. But his delight is in the Law of the LORD, and on His Law, he meditates day and night. He is like a tree planted by streams of water, which yields its fruit in season and whose leaf does not wither. Whatever he does prospers." {Ps.1:1-3}

*Jesus said to him, "You shall love the LORD your God with all your heart, with all your soul, and with all your mind. This is the first and great commandment. "And the second is like it: You shall love your neighbor as yourself. **On these two commandments hang all the Law and the Prophets.**"* {Matthew 22:37-40}

So, if we bind these two commandments on our heart, we will fulfill the entire law. He was not saying, "don't worry about it anymore, I know you can't do it." He instructed us to be filled with His spirit and to no longer walk according to the flesh. We are enabled. We have been given the ability to fulfill the law because His nature is within us. This also means that we are without excuse. By His Spirit living within us, He has written His laws upon our heart. As we commune with Him, we are empowered by His Spirit and enabled to fulfill the law. *"If you really fulfill the royal law according to the Scripture, "You shall love your neighbor as yourself," you do well;"* {James 2:8}

I grew up in a different era. I was a little girl in the 80's, and if I did something I shouldn't have done or if I was in a situation that required a response, my dad would ask me, "What would Jesus do, Tia (that was my nickname)?" Now, if only he had thought to make Christian bracelets and t-shirts back then. I couldn't believe it when I saw the mass marketing for "WWJD" stuff. The Holy Spirit must have shared the same thought with many other believers and then someone decided to market it. If everyone followed this mantra and sincerely thought about "what love would do" before making decisions, the world would be a better place. Asking ourselves this question is a great way to filter our thoughts and actions through a lens of love. If we are acting out of love, we will not sin. Because love is not proud. It does not boast. It is not self-seeking. Love doesn't lie, steal, kill, covet, murder or blaspheme. When we walk according to what love would do, we will fulfill the law. Jesus came to settle our debt from sin, and in doing so, He fulfilled the sacrifices required in the Old Covenant once and for all. He also became our high priest, and He provided us with the indwelling of the Holy Spirit. He made our bodies the tabernacle. He has given us the ability to walk in righteousness and to turn away from desires that are in contradiction to His Word. We are equipped and empowered to do this when we spend time in His Word and when we remain in an active and daily relationship with Him.

Can you see how He has established and fulfilled the law, and He has not destroyed it?

- *"A man who wanders from the way of understanding will rest in the assembly of the dead."* {Prov 21:16}

- *"One who turns away his ear from hearing the law, even his prayer is an abomination."* {Prov 28:9}

- *"Where there is no revelation, the people cast off restraint; But happy is he who keeps the law."* {Prov 29:18}

- *"Open my eyes, that I may see wondrous things from Your law."* {Psalm 119:18}

- *"Praise the Lord! Blessed is the man who fears the Lord, who delights greatly in His commandments."* {Psalm 112:1}

CHAPTER EIGHT

Christ Addresses the 7 Churches in the Book of Revelation

The book of Revelation is full of prophesy revealing the things to come. It begins with seven letters to seven churches. The Holy Spirit inspired John to write each of the seven letters which contain prophetic words from Jesus. Christ revealed the mystery of the seven lampstands in a vision. Jesus said, *"The mystery of the seven stars that you saw in my right hand and of the seven golden lampstands is this: The seven stars are the angels of the seven churches, and the seven lampstands are the seven churches."* {Rev 1:20 NIV}

Revelation begins with an introduction that tells its readers, that the messages it contains were intended to show His followers the things that must shortly take place in the future. Though He addresses each church individually, it can be assumed that the collective representation of each one, is illustrative of all people found within the faith. The message to each church is given at the beginning of a book that prophetically speaks of end- times, God's final battle and judgement of all humanity, and the ultimate reign of His Kingdom on this earth.

Keep in mind that, as followers of Christ, we are the Church. The Church does not consist of mere walls of wood, mortar, and stone. As believers who have the indwelling of the Holy Spirit, our bodies are now the temple of God. In unity, we make up the body of Christ when we come together in fellowship, faith, and worship. As we read these messages to the churches, we must think of them in terms of the seven different categories that characterize people of faith. So, as an individual member of the body of Christ, which group would you fall into? It is important to note, that all the people being addressed are professing faith as believers and followers of Christ. Jesus described each of the churches in this way:

1) The Loveless Church: Revelation 2: 1-7

This church was doing many things right; Christ acknowledged that they were patient, dedicated, determined, disciplined, and discerning. But, as they went along, they ended up straying from their relationship with Him. They were doing some good works, but they had wandered away from their love relationship with the Lord. Jesus had this to say, *"Nevertheless, I have this against you, that you have left your first love."* This church had a heart problem. Everything looked good on the outside, but their hearts were not in the right place. Their commitment to follow the Lord with endurance was dim. He warned them, *"Remember therefore from where you have fallen;* **repent and do the first works, or else** *I will come to you quickly and* **remove your lampstand from its place—unless you repent."**

What does it mean for a Christian to leave their "first love"? It means to "wander away" from the relationship. It describes a love that has become cold.

God doesn't want to become a to-do list. He wants us to love Him and to be in an active relationship with Him. The Lord calls us to repent and do the first works [the fruits of love], or else - else what? "I will remove your lampstand from its place." This is an ultimatum. If a sinner responds, repents, returns to their first love, and does the early works, all is well and good - he will be saved. But ultimately, it is a choice. There is a condition here and a consequence. As you're reading, if you feel like this is describing where you are today in your relationship with Jesus, then repent and return. What did you do when you first became a Christian? What spiritual disciplines did you have that kept you close to Christ and activated you to follow Him? Return to the way you started. If you don't have the desire or the passion, begin praying and asking God, *"Create in me a pure heart, O God, and renew a steadfast spirit within me."* {Psalm 51:10 NIV}

Ask him to give you the "want to."

Jesus made a profound statement to this loveless church. He said, *"But this you have, that you hate **the deeds of the Nicolaitans, which I also hate**."* {Rev 2:6}

This is a curious statement, and so I spent some time researching it. Hate is a strong word, especially for Jesus. The word itself comes from the Greek word miseo which means 'to detest.' Who in the world were the Nicolaitans, and what were their deeds that had raised the ire of Christ?

There are only two references to the Nicolaitans in Scripture. The first is found when Jesus was addressing to the church in Ephesus, and the second is when He addressed the church in Pergamos {Rev 2:6 and Rev 2:15}.

Irenaeus was a Greek cleric who helped develop Christian theology. He died in 202 AD. Clement of Alexandria was a Christian theologian who died in 215 AD. Both Irenaeus and Clement recorded that they considered Nicolas of Antioch to be the founder of the Gnostic sect known as the Nicolaitans. Another early writer, Hippolytus, adds that Nicolas "departed from sound doctrine." Clement claimed that Nicolas became an ascetic and also that his followers later perverted his teachings to encompass idolatry and immorality.

The meaning of the word Nicolaos is "one who conquers the people." But, the meaning of the name may have nothing to do with the Nicolaitan doctrine. If we associate the doctrine that God hated with the meaning of the name, it would only be a wild guess and mere speculation. The only mention found regarding the "deeds" and "doctrines" of the Nicolaitans can be found in the two cities of Ephesus and Pergamum, both of which were pagan and practiced the occult. Both are located in modern-day Turkey. Pergamum was identified as one of the most wicked cities in the history of the ancient world, and its citizens practiced many forms of the occult.

In Ephesus, the leading pagan religion involved the worship of the goddess Artemis. In both cities, believers were intensely and regularly persecuted by those who practiced and followed the pagan religions. Christian citizens were forced to contend with paganism on a level that was well beyond all other cities. Pagan activities were the center of life in these cities, and it was challenging for believers to separate themselves from the culture. These Christians promoted a position of tolerance which ultimately led people to indulge in worldly sins and lowered God's standards in the eyes of men. We cannot compromise with the world and tolerate continued lifestyles of sin in the Church. We have to preach the truth as it is written, from the Bible, for it is not our Word, it is God's. It is not for us to pick and choose the parts we like and don't like.

The "doctrine" of the Nicolaitans seemed to convey that it was not necessary to separate oneself from the world in order to faithfully follow Christ. Essentially, they believed it was acceptable to compromise morality in order to live in harmony with both the Church and the world. This was the "doctrine" of the Nicolaitans that Jesus "hated." This version of faith led to a weak and worldly version of Christianity that was without conviction and lacked power.

In many churches today, believers are being taught that because of the death and grace of Christ, God's law has become meaningless. In other words, regardless of what Scripture teaches, once we have received grace by faith we are no longer expected or required to be doers of the Word. Basically, the pursuit of righteousness and following God's commands is optional. This was the doctrine of the Nicolaitans. The message Christ had for the loveless church ended like this, *"He who has an ear, let him hear what the Spirit says to the churches. **To him who overcomes** I will give to eat from the tree of life, which is in the midst of the Paradise of God."*

2) The Persecuted Church: Revelation 2:8-11

To this church, Christ says, *"I know your works, tribulation, and poverty (but you are rich)"* {Rev 2:9}

He is telling them that He has seen all the hardship, trials and human poverty that they have endured, but in spite of this, this church is spiritually rich. They have stored up their treasures in heaven. When Jesus was with the disciples he told them, *"Do not store up for yourselves treasures on earth, where moths and vermin destroy, and where thieves break in and steal. But store up for yourselves treasures in heaven, where moths and vermin do not destroy, and where thieves do not break in and steal. For where your treasure is, there your heart will be also."* {Matt 6:19-21 NIV}

Today, most Christians think very little about being persecuted for their faith, although that time may be coming. However, there are many places in the world where Christians are persecuted on a daily basis. The Bible says this church suffered because of tribulation, poverty, and persecution. But the Lord says to them, ***"Do not fear*** *any of those things which you are about to suffer…* ***Be faithful until death****, and I will give you the crown of life"* Christ finished his message by saying, *"He who has an ear, let him hear what the Spirit says to the churches.* ***He who overcomes*** *shall not be hurt by the second death."*

Jesus was saying that we must be faithful to the end. We may lose our physical body, but that will be insignificant in comparison to preserving our soul in eternity.

3) The Compromising Church: Revelation 2:12-17

This church was faithful in some areas, but its followers had compromised along the way. Christ said that there are some who were holding up false doctrine and were not staying true to the Word of God. Jesus said there were also some in the church who hold the doctrine of the Nicolaitans, which he hates. He told them that these things are putting a stumbling block in front of His people.

We must pay attention and watch out for a diluted doctrine delivered by charismatic leaders who employ false teachings and omit the full message of the gospel. If that makes us intolerant in the eyes of some, then so be it. As Christians, we must also be committed to speaking the truth in love.

*"...**no longer be infants**, tossed back and forth by the waves, and blown here and there by every wind of teaching and by the cunning and craftiness of people in their deceitful scheming. **Instead**, speaking the truth in love, we will **grow to become in every respect the mature body** of him who is the head, that is, Christ."* {Eph 4:14-15 NIV}

A false belief that some hold is that we just need to have a childlike faith. Ephesians chapter 4 verse 14 begins with this... "No longer be infants." Allow me to wander down a rabbit hole for a moment, and then we can finish reviewing the letters to the churches.

Have you ever heard someone say, "I don't need to worry about all of these doctrinal issues, I just need a childlike faith? Generally, this belief stems from a verse in Matthew 18:3 which says, *"Truly I tell you, unless you change and become like little children, you will never enter the kingdom of heaven."*

Just google the phrase 'childlike faith' and you will find plenty of church websites that use this one verse to establish the fact that we must be like children to enter heaven. Yet, to understand what Jesus actually meant, we must go back to the first verse in chapter 18 and discover why He was having this conversation. *"At that time the **disciples came to Jesus and asked, "Who, then, is the greatest in the kingdom of heaven?"** He called a little child to him, and placed the child among them. And he said: "Truly I tell you, unless you change and become like little children, you will never enter the kingdom*

147

of heaven. Therefore, whoever takes the lowly position of this child is the greatest in the kingdom of heaven." {Matt 18:1-4 NIV}

Jesus was answering their question, which was, "Who then is greatest in the kingdom of heaven?" He was teaching the disciples a lesson in humility. He was encouraging us to be humble like a child. He wasn't advising that we should become childlike. Let's look at Scripture for confirmation. *"When I was a child, I talked like a child, I thought like a child, I reasoned like a child. When I became a man, **I put the ways of childhood behind me.**"* {1 Cor 13:11 NIV}

*"So, let us stop going over the basic teachings about Christ again and again. Let us go on instead and become **mature** in our understanding. Surely, we don't need to start again with the fundamental importance of repenting from evil deeds and placing our faith in God. You don't need further instruction about baptisms, the laying on of hands, the resurrection of the dead, and eternal judgment. And so, God willing, we will move forward to further understanding."* {Heb 6:1-3 -NLT}

*"Like newborn babies, crave pure spiritual milk, so that by it you may **grow up in your salvation**, now that you have tasted that the Lord is good."* {1 Pet 2:2-3 NIV}

Paul wrote a stern warning about our need to mature and grow in our spiritual understanding. This is what he had to say: *"We have much to say about this, but it is hard to make it clear to you because you no longer try to understand. In fact, though by this time you ought to be teachers, you need someone to teach you the elementary truths of God's word all over again. You need milk, not solid food! **Anyone who lives on milk, being still an infant, is not acquainted with the teaching about righteousness.** But **solid food is for the mature**, who by constant use* *have trained themselves to distinguish good from evil."* {Hebrews 5: 11-14 NIV}

Back to the churches...

4) The Corrupt Church: Revelations 2:18-29

Christ begins His message by acknowledging that He is familiar with the works, love, service, faith and the patience of this church. Although, He also says, *"Nevertheless, I have this against you: You tolerate that woman Jezebel, who calls herself a prophet. By her teaching* **she misleads my servants** *into sexual immorality ... I* **have given her time to repent of her immorality, but she is unwilling."** {Rev 2:20-21 NIV}

As it relates to moral boundaries and spiritual disciplines, many churches and professing Christians are compromising the Word of God in an effort to be culturally relevant and all-inclusive. Certainly, being morally inclusive is the quickest way to fill the pews, right? Jesus concluded the message to this church by saying, *"but hold fast what you have till I come. And he who overcomes, and keeps My works until the end,"* Christ promised that if we are faithful and hold fast without compromise, we will reign with Him.

We cannot overlook immorality and deem that it is acceptable or even tolerable to the Lord, especially in His Holy Sanctuary. He has clearly told us that sin is detestable to Him. Although the Lord hates sin, this does not mean that we should not love people despite their sin. It means that we cannot create an atmosphere of tolerance for the behaviors that are offensive to the Lord.

We must rely on and continually point to God's Word to define the uncompromising standards of our faith. Each and every person, regardless of their story, is deeply and unconditionally loved by God. However, we all battle with a terminal illness called sin. Some people struggle with sins which they feel have overtaken them to the degree that they believe they were born with a natural tendency. I agree. It can be difficult and confusing to struggle with something that feels natural but is in contradiction with the Word of God. After all, God made each of us. So, how is it, that we have been created with a particular tendency, yet the desire that we can't seem to control is defined in God's Word as sin?

Each one of us has some sort of pre-genetic disposition towards a particular type of sin. However, my struggle with sin will be different than yours. Some people struggle with addictions to drugs, alcohol and pornography. Some lie and some gossip. Some people struggle with greed, vanity, jealousy, selfish ambition and even pride. The list could go on and on. *"Do you not know that the unrighteous will not inherit the kingdom of God? Do not be deceived. Neither fornicators, nor idolaters, nor adulterers, nor homosexuals, nor sodomites, nor thieves, nor covetous, nor drunkards, nor revilers, nor extortioners will inherit the kingdom of God. And such were some of you. But you were washed, but you were sanctified, but you were justified in the name of the Lord Jesus and by the Spirit of our God."* {1 Cor 6:9-11}

Some sins are private; some are very public and obvious. We all struggle with some type of sin, and it is only by the power of the Holy Spirit that we can overcome the dominion of sin in our lives. If we have a natural desire to do something that is contrary to God's Word, it does not make that "something" acceptable. We can be freed from sin and delivered

150

from our transgressions when we pursue a genuine relationship with the Lord and ask Him for His help. Through faith in Jesus Christ, we are not only freed from the penalty of sin, we are also freed from the power of sin over us. One of the marks of a genuine relationship with Christ, is a desire to be obedient to His teachings.

The Scriptures define God's standard and they guide us toward change, it is not the other way around. *"Keep your servant also from willful sins; **may they not rule over me**. Then I will be blameless, innocent of great transgression."* {Psalm 19:13 NIV}

To begin our journey of faith, we cannot start with excuses; we start by acknowledging that we are sinners that need a Savior. There is nothing that any of us have done that cannot be purified by what Jesus has done for us. He will gather our heap of ashes from the broken pieces of our hearts and lives, and He will turn it into something beautiful.

5) The Dead Church: Revelations 3:1-6

*"I know all the things you do, and that you have a reputation for being alive—but you are dead. <u>**Wake up!**</u> **Strengthen what little remains, for even what is left is almost dead.** I find that **your actions do not meet the requirements of my God.** Go back to what you heard and believed at first; hold to it firmly. Repent and turn to me again. **If you don't wake up, I will come to you suddenly,** as unexpected as a thief. "Yet **there are some in the church** in Sardis **who have not soiled their clothes with evil.** They will walk with me in white, for they are worthy. **All who are victorious** will be clothed in white. **I will never erase their names from the Book of Life,** but I will announce*

151

before my Father and his angels that they are mine." {Rev 3:1-5 NLT}

This is huge. These people are physically alive, but they are spiritually dead. When He says the words, "All who are victorious," what is He referring to? What are they victorious over? Persecution, forsaking one's self, and the desires of the flesh, all for the prize of eternal life. Jesus is saying that the one who has "overcome" is the one who will be clothed in white garments and that He will not **ERASE** their name from the Book of Life. If a name is going to get erased, wouldn't it have already been written in the Book? This is a church full of casual or misguided Christians.

Let's visit a few additional verses that mention "blotting out" names.

- *Then the LORD said to Moses, "Write this on a scroll as something to be remembered and make sure that Joshua hears it because **I will completely blot out the** name of Amalek from under heaven."* {Exodus 17:14 NIV}

- *The LORD replied to Moses, "Whoever has sinned against me **I will blot out of my book**."* {Exodus 32:33 NIV}

- *"The LORD will never be willing to forgive them; his wrath and zeal will burn against them. All the curses written in this book will fall on them, and **the LORD will blot out their names** from under heaven."* {Duet 29:20 NIV}

6) The Faithful Church: Revelations 3:7-13

*"I know your works. See, I have set before you an open door, and no one can shut it; for you have a little strength, have kept My word, and have not denied My name...**Because you have kept My command to persevere**, I also will keep you from the hour of trial which shall come upon the whole world, to test those who dwell on the earth. Behold, I am coming quickly! **Hold fast what you have, that no one may take your crown. <u>He who overcomes</u>**, I will make him a pillar in the temple of My God,"* {Rev 3:8,10-12}

The Lord is saying that He has set an open door for ministry in the hearts of the people that possess this kind of faithfulness. These are those who depend on the Word of God and His faithfulness to strengthen the body when and where needed. These believers are faithful and will work to build His Church according to His ways and not their own. Being faithful to God's Word will lead to open doors for ministry. When His Word is the foundation, then everything else will line up in its place. We are encouraged to boldly proclaim our faith in Christ and the full gospel, regardless of the cost. We should be diligent and serious about keeping the commands, and we must persevere.

According to Merriam-Webster's definition, to persevere means to "persist in a state, enterprise, or undertaking in spite of counter influences, opposition, or discouragement."

7) The Lukewarm Church: Revelations 3:14-22

*"I know your deeds, that you are neither cold nor hot. **I wish you were either one or the other! So, because you are lukewarm—neither hot nor cold—I am about to spit you out of my mouth.** You say, 'I am rich; I have acquired wealth and do not need a thing.' But you do not realize that*

you are wretched, pitiful, poor, blind and naked. I counsel you to buy from me gold refined in the fire, so you can become rich; and white clothes to wear, so you can cover your shameful nakedness; and salve to put on your eyes, so you can see. **Those whom I love I rebuke and discipline. So be earnest and repent.** *Here I am! I stand at the door and knock. If anyone hears my voice and opens the door, I will come in and eat with that person, and they with me... Whoever has ears, let them hear what the Spirit says to the churches."* {Rev 3:15-20,22 NIV}

These people literally make the Lord sick. These are worldly people that are both arrogant and prideful. The nakedness that is being referred to here is actually a metaphor for spiritual nakedness. This verse is also using eye salve as a metaphor for genuine repentance, which is the only thing that can restore our spiritual eyesight. God loves us even when we cannot see, and He counsels us to "be zealous and repent" when it's needed. Even when we push Him away, He stands at the door and knocks, hoping and waiting to be invited back in. These are the words of the Lord, "I wish you were cold or hot." He is not interested in our casual and comfortable Christianity.

Lukewarm is not ok. He wants one or the other; we either love Him or we don't. We serve Him, or we serve ourselves. Indifference is still a choice; it just moves us in the wrong direction.

At the end of point # 3
read I CoR. 10: 1-13
and Jude 5

CHAPTER NINE

Misunderstood

Through my research, I have compiled most, if not all, of the primary verses that are typically used to articulate the Christian views on the topic of "Eternal Security." Let's consider them together:

1) *"And I give them eternal life, and they shall never perish; neither shall anyone snatch them out of My hand. "My Father, who has given them to Me, is greater than all; and no one is able to snatch them out of My Father's hand."* {John 10:28-29}

We don't lose our free will when we gain our salvation. The Apostle James has warned us not to be a "wanderer from the truth." {James 5:19-20} We can choose to reject the Lord by rejecting His teachings, and we can walk away and depart from the truth. If this occurs, no one snatched me. I left. In fact, do you recall the verse about rejecting the call to holiness? It said that if we reject the call to holiness that we are not rejecting man, we are rejecting God. I can willfully choose to follow my own worldly desires.

As we have repeatedly established, reading the Scripture in context is critical. So again, let's determine why Jesus made this statement in the first place. In this case, He was responding to a group of people that were questioning whether He was the promised Messiah. The answer He gave (found in verses 28 and 29) was in response to a question: *"The Jews who were there gathered around him, saying, "How long will you keep us in suspense? If you are the Messiah, tell us plainly."* {John 10:24 NIV}

Jesus is answering them to establish recognition of His identity and to help them understand the power of God. He wasn't answering a question on the topic of eternal security. He was pointing out that His authentic followers would spiritually discern His identity as the Messiah, and that no one could sway His followers from their conviction. Jesus also stated that the only way someone could understand His identity is if His Father was leading them.

Although this Scripture is touted as a validation for eternal security, nowhere in the verse did Jesus say that His followers cannot lose their salvation. I would also contend that if we find even one Scripture that contradicts the teaching of eternal security, it should cause us to diligently search the Word of God to be sure we are abiding in truth. Paul spoke about our freedom in Christ and also our Christian Liberty. He said, *"Stand fast therefore in the liberty by which Christ has made us free, and **do not be entangled again** with a yoke of bondage. Indeed I, Paul, say to you that if you become circumcised, Christ will profit you nothing. And I testify again to every man who becomes circumcised that he is a debtor to keep the whole law. **You have become estranged from Christ, you who attempt to be justified by law; you have fallen from grace.** For we through the Spirit eagerly wait for the hope of **righteousness by faith.** For in Christ Jesus neither circumcision nor uncircumcision avails anything, but faith working through love."* {Gal 5:1-6}

Paul wrote the book of Galatians while he was in Rome around 68 AD. He was writing to help prevent the Galatians from further backsliding. The Galatians were teaching that justification and reconciliation with God could be achieved merely by following the law and the requirements of the Old Covenant. Paul was explaining the relation of Christians of the New Covenant with the Jews of the Old Covenant. He was saying that all who choose to go back and rely solely on the law, are then under obligation to fulfill the entire law. His point was that our justification is by faith in Jesus Christ alone, without the works of the law. If we look back into Chapters 1 and 2 in the book of Galatians, we can see the intent of his message.

The verses about our freedom in Christ are often misunderstood, as are the passages that reference the constant warfare between the flesh and the spirit. Some take these verses to infer that we are victims of the flesh and are helpless to live right. That was not the message spoken by Paul. The people of Paul's day were not all convinced that faith in Christ was sufficient, and some were "falling away," back to the covenant rituals. Faith in Christ seemed too simple a concept. The Galatians believed circumcision to be a ritualistic act that demonstrated their love for and commitment to God. Even though it was painful, they considered it a worthy practice and believed that it would make them more spiritual. The Galatians did not understand that by maintaining the ritual of circumcision, they were actually incurring irrevocable contractual obligations. Paul was diligently trying to convince them that by keeping to the rituals of the Old Covenant, they had nothing to gain, and everything to lose.

"I am astonished that you are so quickly deserting the one who called you to live in the grace of Christ and

are turning to a different gospel— which is really no gospel at all. Evidently some people are throwing you into confusion and are trying to pervert the gospel of Christ. But even if we or an angel from heaven should preach a gospel other than the one we preached to you, let them be under God's curse!" {Gal 1:6-8 NIV}

*"When **I saw that they were not acting in line with the truth of the gospel,** I said to Cephas in front of them all, "You are a Jew, yet you live like a Gentile and not like a Jew. How is it, then, that you force Gentiles to follow Jewish customs? "We who are Jews by birth and not sinful Gentiles **know that a person is not justified by the works of the law, but by faith in Jesus Christ.** So we, too, have put our faith in Christ Jesus that we may be justified by faith in Christ and not by the works of the law, because by the works of the law no one will be justified. "**But if, in seeking to be justified in Christ, we Jews find ourselves also among the sinners, doesn't that mean that Christ promotes sin? Absolutely not! If I rebuild what I destroyed, then I really would be a lawbreaker.** "For through the law I died to the law so that I might live for God. I have been crucified with Christ and I no longer live, but Christ lives in me. The life I now live in the body, I live by faith in the Son of God, who loved me and gave himself for me. **I do not set aside the grace of God,** for if righteousness could be gained through the law, Christ died for nothing!"* {Gal 2:14-21 NIV}

Paul was trying to reason with the Galatians. He wanted them to clearly understand that they are not justified by works, period. He is reasoning with them hoping they would realize the truth and accept that Jesus was and is the final sacrifice for the remission of sins.

"If we confess our sins, he is faithful and just and will forgive us our sins and purify us from all unrighteousness." {1

John 1:9 NIV} Paul continues in Galatians chapter 3 by saying…

*"Beware, brethren, lest there be in any of you an evil heart of unbelief, in **departing from the living God**; but exhort one another daily, while it is called "Today," lest any of you be hardened through the deceitfulness of sin. For we have become **partakers of Christ if we hold the beginning of our confidence steadfast to the end.**"* {Heb 3:12-14}

Paul is specifically referring to believers in these verses. Unbelievers are certainly not advised to "exhort one another daily." Neither can they revert to sin and depart from the living God, for sinners are estranged from God until they repent and believe. Jesus said, *"But **the one who endures to the end** will be saved."* {Matt 24:13 NLT}

Paul gave some recommendations.

He said, *"Pursue peace with all people, and holiness, without which no one will see the Lord: **looking carefully lest anyone fall short of the grace of God**; lest any root of bitterness springing up cause trouble, and by this many become defiled;"* {Hebrews 12:14-15}

2) *"Keep your lives free from the love of money and be content with what you have, because God has said, "Never will I leave you; never will I forsake you."* {Hebrews 13:5 NIV}

This verse does not say that it is impossible for "us" to lose the gift of salvation by leaving or forsaking God. It says that He won't leave or forsake us. He gives us a guarantee which is evidenced by His Holy Spirit. It's like a reservation or a deposit on our future inheritance. However, until we physically die, we've not yet obtained the inheritance. To receive it, we must endure to the end. God's love for us is without condition, however, His promises are conditional. His promises are based on our love for Him. He demonstrates this when He says, I will do this, IF, you do this.

Several verses confirm that we can be assured of our salvation, as long as we do not ultimately reject God by continued disregard, or by our deliberate disobedience. If we disregard the Word of God and in our rebellion, we practice deliberate disobedience, we will ultimately separate ourselves from fellowship with Christ. If we are walking according to the Spirit, we do not need to live in fear of our eternal destiny. If we will remain in the process, we can have confident hope that the Lord will see us through. And this is what Paul meant when he said, *"...being confident of this, that he who began a good work in you will carry it on to completion until the day of Christ Jesus."* {Phil 1:6}

What about Predestination?

3) *"For those God foreknew he also predestined to be conformed to the image of his Son, that he might be the firstborn among many brothers and sisters. And those he predestined, he also called; those he called, he also justified; those he justified, he also glorified."* {Rom 8: 29-30 NIV}

Does this mean that a "predestined" person has no choice but to enter the Kingdom of God? No, it does not! The term "predestination" simply suggests that God has predetermined the destiny of those He calls, but it does not indicate that He predetermines whether they actually will remain faithful to their calling. Does "foreknowledge" suggest that at the beginning of time that God determined exactly who would be saved and who wouldn't? No! It simply suggests that God knew us before we knew Him, that His knowing us was an essential key to our knowing Him.

Let's consider the story of Moses. God said, "*I am the Lord. I appeared to Abraham, to Isaac, and to Jacob as God Almighty, but by my name the Lord, I did not make myself fully known to them. I also established my covenant with them to give them the land of Canaan, where they resided as foreigners.*" The Lord told Moses to give the Israelites this message from Him, "*...and I will bring you to the land I swore with uplifted hand to give to Abraham, to Isaac, and to Jacob. I will give it to you as a possession. I am the Lord.*" {Exodus 6:3-8 NIV}

But, God never promised that He would bring people, no matter what. People were expected to obey God. Moses led God's people for many years, but God did not lead them straight into the land that He had promised them. The trip from Egypt to Canaan should have taken just months, but instead, they wandered in the desert for 40 years. Why? Quite simply, because the Israelites did not obey God while they were wandering in the wilderness. But during the entire time, God had provided for their needs, as He does for ours to this day.

"Yet the Lord says, "During the forty years that I led you through the wilderness, your clothes did not wear out, nor did the sandals on your feet. You ate no bread and drank no wine or other fermented drink. I did this so that you might know that I am the Lord your God." {Duet 29:5-6 NIV}

After being delivered from Egypt, the Israelites soon began complaining about God and His provisions for them. I am going to paraphrase the Lord's response. So, in return, God said that none of these ignorant, and disobedient complainers would enter the promised land, except Joshua and Caleb. The forty years of wandering was to wait on the entire generation of Israelites, whom God had mercifully delivered from slavery, to die. True to His Word and because of the Israelites disobedience, out of all the men over 20 years old at the time of God's proclamation, only Joshua and Caleb would see the land. {Num 32:11-12} Why? Because only Joshua and Caleb had followed God, fully and faithfully.

*"Nevertheless, as surely as I live and as surely as the glory of the Lord fills the whole earth, not one of those who saw my glory and the signs I performed in Egypt and in the wilderness but who disobeyed me and tested me ten times— not one of them will ever see the land I promised on oath to their ancestors. No one who has treated me with contempt will ever see it. But because my servant Caleb has a different spirit and follows me wholeheartedly, I will bring him into the land he went to, and his descendants will inherit it... **Not one of you will enter the land I swore with uplifted hand to make your home**, except Caleb, son of Jephunneh and Joshua son of Nun."* {Num 14:21-24,30 NIV}

Aaron and Moses had led the Israelites for years after their emancipation from Egypt, and they basically did what God had commanded them to do. However, there was a time when their frustration with the people became unbearable. Aaron and Moses were so upset with the people, they made it appear as if they, by their own power, were providing water for the Israelites. *"Hear now, you rebels! Must <u>we</u> bring water for you out of this rock?"* {Numbers 20:10}

Moses and Aaron did not give honor to God by acknowledging Him. Because of their sin, they suffered a consequence and they lost the blessing of entering the land that God had promised them. How many times do we not give God the credit He deserves? How many

162

blessings do we miss out on because we are not faithful or humble?

*"But the Lord said to Moses and Aaron, "**Because you did not trust in me enough to honor me as holy** in the sight of the Israelites, **you will not** bring this community into the land I give them."* {Numbers 20:12 NIV}

Before Moses died, he was allowed to view the panorama of the land God promised. The Lord said to him, *"This is the land I promised on oath to Abraham, Isaac, and Jacob when I said, 'I will give it to your descendants.' I have let you see it with your eyes, but you will not cross over into it." And Moses the servant of the Lord died there in Moab, as the Lord had said."* {Duet 34:4-5}

When a family plans a vacation, they choose a pre-determined location for their travels and they are usually set to arrive within a specific time-frame. In other words, they are now "pre-destined" to show up at their planned location. It is entirely possible that the family could have an accident on their way, or they could be re-routed. It is a sad reality, but they may not reach their intended destination. In the same way, it is possible for those "predestined" to God's Kingdom to "fall away" and never reach the destination God had intended for them. Just in case you may be thinking that the stories of God in the Old Testament are not relevant today, we should not forget that God does not change. He is the same God in the Old Testament that He is in the New Testament. *"But the Lord's plans stand firm forever; his intentions can never be shaken."* {Psalm 33:11 NLT}

"Jesus Christ is the same yesterday and today and forever." {Hebrews 13:8 NIV}

4) *"And do not grieve the Holy Spirit of God, with whom you were sealed for the day of redemption."* {Ephesians 4:30 NIV}

Salvation is reserved for us in heaven. Think of the original intent of a seal. The original purpose of a seal is to authenticate something. You have been marked for, *"...an inheritance incorruptible and undefiled and that does not fade away, reserved in heaven for you"* {1 Peter 1:3-4}

But, we don't actually attain it until we have stood firm in our faith and endured to the very end. *"But the one who endures to the end will be saved."* {Matt 24:13 NLT} *"If we endure, we shall also reign with Him. If we deny Him, He also will deny us."* {2 Tim 2:12}

As it relates to salvation and eternal life, we have a future inheritance, but we do yet possess eternal salvation. We have a confirmed reservation in heaven. Listen to what Paul said, *"Brothers and sisters, I do not consider myself yet to have taken hold of it. But one thing I do: Forgetting what is behind and straining toward what is ahead, I press on toward the goal to win the prize for which God has called me heavenward in Christ Jesus."* {Phil 3:13-14 NIV}

Paul is saying that he did not think of himself as having already obtained his salvation. We are marked for salvation, and if we endure to the end with God's help, it will be as if we were in fact "saved" from our conversion. It's humbling to think about the fact that Paul questioned whether or not he had obtained eternal salvation. Paul wrote much of the New Testament and was persecuted for his faith. Has anyone been truer to the Word of God. Perhaps, even more humbling is the fact that Moses wasn't allowed to set foot

164

into the "promised land" because of his disobedience. I mean, Moses led these people out of Egypt and wandered in the wilderness for 40 years with folks that griped at him for decades. Other than God, has anyone been more faithful and patient? God holds us all to a high standard. Father help us to be faithful and help us to endure.

In Ephesians, it is important to note that Paul is writing to the believers in Ephesus, not to unbelievers. The Ephesians were primarily non-Jewish followers of Christ. He begins to admonish them, *"But fornication and all uncleanness or covetousness, **let it not even be named among you**, as is fitting for saints; neither filthiness, nor foolish talking, nor coarse jesting, which are not fitting, but rather giving of thanks. For this you know, that no fornicator, unclean person, nor covetous man, who is an idolater, has any inheritance in the kingdom of Christ and God. **Let no one deceive you with empty words**, for because of these things **the wrath of God comes upon the sons of disobedience**. Therefore, do not be partakers with them. For you were once darkness, but now you are light in the Lord. Walk as children of light."* {Eph 5:3-8}

The Holy Spirit has three distinct ways of bringing revelation to us:

1) by exposing our guilt,

2) by illuminating the word of God, and

3) by revealing Christ to us.

*"You stiff-necked people! Your hearts and ears are still uncircumcised. **You are just like your ancestors: You always resist the Holy Spirit!** Was there ever a prophet your ancestors did not persecute? They even killed those who predicted the coming of the Righteous One. And now you*

have betrayed and murdered him— you who have received the law that was given through angels but have not obeyed it." {Acts 7:51-54 NIV}

It is the Spirit of God that reveals the truth of His Word; He does not lead us away from it. We can only receive discernment of spiritual things by and through the Spirit. God will show us our sin, but He will never excuse it. He will not allow us to rationalize our lack of self-control. Repentance is a vital part of our process of sanctification, and thus, we are called to it. *"For by one sacrifice he has made perfect forever those **who are being made holy.**"* {Heb 10:14 NIV}

This verse exemplifies the fact that Jesus being the single sacrifice was indeed "once and for all," in the truest sense of the words. His death on the cross was sufficient to cover all past, current and future sins. This single sacrifice is for those who are "being sanctified." The "sanctified" refers to those who remain in him. The offering is for those who, through continued repentance and fellowship, remain steadfast and endure with Him. As long as we have breath in our lungs, we have an opportunity to turn back to Him, even if we have turned away. Through our sincere repentance, we can be restored to righteousness in Christ.

5) *"he saved us, not because of righteous things we had done, but because of his mercy. He saved us through the washing of rebirth and renewal by the Holy Spirit,"* {Titus 3:5 NIV}

When a person puts their faith in Christ as Lord, they are regenerated as a new creation. I've heard some assert that "if a Christian lost their salvation, they would have to be un-generated, and the Bible doesn't give any evidence that the new birth can be taken away." As we've seen, many verses throughout Scripture warn of the consequences of "wandering or falling away."

6) *"...the Spirit of truth. The world cannot accept him, because it neither sees him nor knows him. But you know him, for he lives with you and will be in you."* {John 14:17 NIV}

"You, however, are not in the realm of the flesh but are in the realm of the Spirit, if indeed the Spirit of God lives in you. And if anyone does not have the Spirit of Christ, they do not belong to Christ." {Romans 8:9 NIV}

What about the Holy Spirit who indwells all believers? As previously mentioned, a believer is sealed until the day of redemption. The Holy Spirit will never leave or forsake you. This is the loving kindness and the faithfulness of our God. He says that it is "His will" that none should perish, but that all should come to repentance. According to Scripture, He will not detach us from His Spirit while there is still breath in our earthly bodies. Even if we "wander from the truth," He continues to whisper to our hearts, and He will stand at the door and knock. *"I the Lord search the heart and examine the mind, to reward each person according to their conduct, according to what their deeds deserve."* {Jer 17:10 NIV}

"For the LORD does not see as man sees; for man looks at the outward appearance, but the LORD looks at the heart." {1 Sam 16:7}

7) Scripture says, *"For I am convinced that neither death nor life, neither angels nor demons, neither the present nor the future, nor any powers, neither height nor depth, nor anything else in all creation, will be able to separate*

us from the love of God that is in Christ Jesus our Lord."
{Romans 8:38-39 NIV}

We must remain in Christ to stay secure. Quality time together is key to any lasting relationship. Time spent together is vital for ensuring healthy marriages, forging strong bonds with our children and developing intimate friendships. Our relationship with Jesus is no different. He must remain on the throne of our life. Everything described in this verse is an external force and there is nothing that can separate us from the love of God, it can only happen by our choice.

8) *"And, on some have compassion, making a distinction; but others save with fear, pulling them out of the fire, hating even the garment defiled by the flesh. Now to Him who is able to keep you from stumbling, And to present you faultless Before the presence of His glory with exceeding joy, To God our Savior, Who alone is wise, Be glory and majesty, Dominion and power, Both now and forever. Amen."* {Jude 23-25}

Yes, by the power of His Spirit dwelling in us, He is able to keep us from stumbling. However, we must cooperate with Him. We have a responsibility to live our lives in accordance with the Word of God. We are righteous because Christ dwells in us and has paid our debt. If we are walking according to the Spirit in our daily lives, we will be convicted when we sin, and the conviction will cause us to repent regularly. When our heart is fixed on Jesus, He is able to present us faultless, our righteousness is obtained through Him.

Would you agree that an omission is a lie? Scripture is used out of context every day. An omission makes it difficult for someone to make wise and accurate evaluations. Thus, to omit material information is

168

deception. For example, have you ever heard this verse? *"There is therefore now no condemnation to those who are in Christ Jesus,"* {Romans 8:1} If you are familiar with the verse, you may also realize that this is only a portion of it. This is the "feel good" part. Years ago, I was attending a church service, and this verse was used to encourage the congregation. I was concerned because the pastor had basically just told everyone in the service that, as believers, we were under no condemnation. Period. But, let's look again. There is a problem with sharing this verse but stopping mid-way. The issue lies in the fact that this statement ends with a comma, not a period.

There is another point being made in the same sentence. Whether intentional or not, it is misleading to stop there. When one hears only the first part of the verse, it sounds good. It sounds easy. Who could or would argue against it? It is a powerful verse, full of hope. However, it is misleading because that is not the full message of the verse. To provide context, let's read all of it. Only then, can we determine its intended meaning. *"There is therefore now no condemnation to those who are in Christ Jesus, **who do not walk according to the flesh**, but according to the Spirit."* {Romans 8:1}

The critical part of this verse mentions walking according to the flesh and it is often omitted, yet it is a pivotal part of the verse. When we hear the full verse, we understand there is a requirement of us and that the promise is contingent on our walk with Him. There is no license for total liberty. Nor is there an offer of eternal security for those who continue in their sin with no regard for pursuing a relationship with the Lord, or who refuse to follow His commands. God will not be mocked. We will reap what we sow.

9) *"They went out from us, but they were not of us; for if they had been of us, they would have continued with us; but they went out that they might be made manifest, that none of them were of us."* {1 John 2:19}

It is common to hear the following assertions within the community of faith… "If one has professed to be saved, but later in life, they return to living life on their own terms, and they show no evidence of a continued relationship with God, then they were probably never saved in the first place. Therefore, 'they were not of us'…or they would have continued with us." Once again, the context in which John was speaking is vital to understanding what he meant. In this passage, John was referring to false teachers. He actually calls them "antichrists" in verse 18. In the verses that precede or follow verse 19 there is not any mention of one who has wandered from the faith.

Let's review the context. These traveling teachers had been part of the original Church in Jerusalem, but they left the Church due to doctrinal differences. They were traveling to churches outside of Jerusalem and trying to win congregations over by touting their false beliefs. The expression Paul used stating "they were not of us" meant that these false teachers were not like John relative to their beliefs. They were teaching different doctrines.

I fully believe there are a tremendous number of professing "Christians" who are not actually saved. Yet, nowhere does the Bible tell us that if a professing Christian "falls away" from his faith, that he was never saved in the first place. If that were the case, then why would Jesus and the disciples have given numerous and stern warnings about the perils of wandering or falling away. Jesus also spoke of our need to overcome the desires of our flesh and the importance of remaining steadfast till the end, at the risk of losing our crown. If you are in the camp that believes that people who fall away or go back to willful sinning were never truly saved, then I want to ask you to consider someone else from the Bible. He is one of God's most beloved, and he is one of the best-known figures in Scripture. The Lord declared him to be "a man after his own heart." That man was King David.

Because of King Saul's disobedience, the Lord removed Him as King. *"And when He had removed him, He raised up for them David as king, to whom also He gave testimony and said, 'I have found David the son of Jesse, a **man after My own heart, who will do all My will.**"* {Acts 13:22}

This new King was actually David the Shepard boy. David had defeated Goliath, the Philistine giant, with just a slingshot and a stone. To help us get to the point, I am going to summarize some of his story, but to do so, we'll need to start with David as a child. As a young boy, David was overheard speaking about Goliath, so King Saul summoned him. At the conclusion of their conversation, Saul told David,

"You are not able to go out against this Philistine and fight him; you are only a young man, and he has been a warrior from his youth. But David said to Saul, "Your servant has been keeping his father's sheep. When a lion or a bear came and carried off a sheep from the flock, I went after it, struck it and rescued the sheep from its mouth. When it turned on me, I seized it by its hair, struck it and killed it. Your servant has killed both the lion and the bear; this uncircumcised Philistine will be like one of them, because he has defied the armies of the living God. The LORD who rescued me from the paw of the lion and the paw of the bear will rescue me from the hand of this Philistine." Saul said to

David, *"Go, and the* LORD *be with you."* {1 Sam 17:33-37 NIV}

So, David readied himself to meet Goliath. Saul attempted to provide David with a coat of armor, but David refused it because it was ill-fitting and heavy. *"Then he took his staff in his hand, chose five smooth stones from the stream, put them in the pouch of his shepherd's bag and, with his sling in his hand, approached the Philistine...He looked David over and saw that he was little more than a boy, glowing with health and handsome, and he despised him. He said to David, "Am I a dog, that you come at me with sticks?" And the Philistine cursed David by his gods. "Come here," he said, "and I'll give your flesh to the birds and the wild animals!" David said to the Philistine, "You come against me with sword and spear and javelin, but* **I come against you in the name of the LORD Almighty, the God of the armies of Israel, whom you have defied. This day the LORD will deliver you into my hands,** *and I'll strike you down and cut off your head. This very day I will give the carcasses of the Philistine army to the birds and the wild animals,* **and the whole world will know that there is a God in Israel. All those gathered here will know that it is not by sword or spear that the LORD saves; for the battle is the LORD's,** *and he will give all of you into our hands." As the Philistine moved closer to attack him, David ran quickly toward the battle line to meet him. Reaching into his bag and taking out a stone, he slung it and struck the Philistine on the forehead. The stone sank into his forehead, and he fell face down on the ground."* {1 Sam 17:40,42-49 NIV}

David had an undeniable relationship with God and an unyielding faith from the time he was a young boy. In fact, if we look back to 1 Samuel chapter 16, Samuel, the prophet of the Lord, was instructed by God to anoint David.

"So, he sent and brought him in. Now he was ruddy, with bright eyes, and good-looking. And the Lord said, "Arise, anoint him; for this is the one!" Then Samuel took the horn of oil and anointed him in the midst of his brothers; and the Spirit of the Lord came upon David from that day forward." {1 Sam 16:12-13}

The Bible clearly tells us that David was chosen by God. He was anointed, and he was indwelt by the Holy Spirit. Now that we have established this, let's go a little further. Before David was appointed King, he found himself hiding in caves and running for his life from King Saul. Saul had become jealous of David because David was honored by the people. So, Saul set out to kill him. While David was running for his life, he wrote this: *"My heart is steadfast, O God, my heart is steadfast; I will sing and give praise."* {Psalm 57:7} Despite his circumstances, David had fixed his heart on the Lord. Many of David's prayers found in Psalms were written after he became King, and we can plainly see how much he trusted in the Lord. David was wholly devoted to serving God because He loved Him. However, David had free-will. David had willfully and blatantly committed a number of grievous sins. He did this despite a powerful relationship with the Lord, and despite the indwelling of the Holy Spirit.

"One evening David got up from his bed and walked around on the roof of the palace. From the roof he saw a woman bathing. The woman was very beautiful, and David sent someone to find out about her. The man said, "She is Bathsheba, the daughter of Eliam and the wife of Uriah the Hittite." Then David sent messengers to get her. She came to him, and he slept with her. (Now she was purifying herself from her monthly uncleanness.) Then she went back home. The woman conceived and sent word to David, saying, "I am pregnant." {2 Sam 11:2-5 NIV}

Scripture says that David sent for her husband, Uriah, who had been in battle. David attempted to get him to return home, in the hopes that Uriah would sleep with his wife. This way, her pregnancy wouldn't be a big surprise. But, Uriah was a loyal man. He didn't want to enjoy the luxuries of home while his troops remained in battle. So, Uriah refused to visit his home. David asked him to stay another day before returning to battle. He got Uriah drunk, thinking that as a result of his intoxication, Uriah might go home and lay with his wife. However, Uriah still did not return home. So, the next morning, David sent word to the head of his military. He ordered a command for Uriah to be placed on the front lines of battle. David instructed his troops to withdraw from Uriah, so he would be struck down by the enemy. His plan was successful, and Uriah was killed. The story ends like this; *"When Uriah's wife heard that her husband was dead, she mourned for him. After the time of mourning was over, David had her brought to his house, and she became his wife and bore him a son. But the thing David had done displeased the Lord."* {2 Sam 11:26-27 NIV}

David, the man after God's own heart, the man who had the indwelling of the Holy Spirit, became an adulterer and a murderer. David repented, as recorded in his prayer found in Psalm 51. The Lord forgives David, but he would still experience the consequences of his sin. The baby conceived by Bathsheba would die, and "the sword would never leave David's house," meaning that he would always have strife. The prophet Nathan explains to David that because of his sin, "he has given the enemies of the Lord great occasion to blaspheme."

As children of God, our sin may become a stumbling block for others. Our sins cause some to question their faith because of our hypocrisy. This is always the tragic result of sin when it is displayed to an onlooking world. For David, grace prevailed over judgment as he approached the Lord with a humble and repentant heart. He was sorrowful over his sin. He did not make excuses. He confessed, and he received correction. He then turned away from his lifestyle of willful sin. In comparison, King Saul had also been anointed, and he, too, sinned against God. Saul had elevated himself to the office of priest, and he made an unlawful sacrifice. Because Saul feared the people's reaction, he disobeyed God by not destroying all the plunder from a captured foe, as he had been instructed by the Lord. And, as if that weren't enough, Saul even built a monument to himself. Geez!

If we analyzed Saul's sin what do you think we would find as the root problem? My guess would be Pride. Pride is a dangerous weapon that can bring us down. The Bible says, "Pride comes before the fall." We need to be on guard against pride. That crafty devil will plant thoughts in our mind. This is why the Bible tells us to take every thought captive and bring it into submission with the Word of God. The enemy of our soul will help and encourage us to exalt and bring glory to ourselves. In reality, we should remain humble and recognize that if we have been given authority or if we are blessed, it is only because of the Lord. He, alone, deserves the glory and the honor.

Let's get back to King Saul…

Silence was Saul's first response to the prophet Samuel's rebuke. In contrast, David's response was one of genuine repentance. Saul's second response to Samuel's rebuke was resistance, followed by a reluctant confession. He was trying to justify his actions as Godly disobedience by claiming that his actions were warranted by the circumstances. In 1 Sam 15:13, we see that Saul was trying to re-position his dis-obedience as righteous defiance. Saul failed to take the personal responsibility for his wrongs, and he tried to pass his guilt off to others {1 Sam 15:24}. He did not seem to be concerned with the cause of his sin, or even the cure. The only real concern Saul had was that his suffering was minimized {1 Sam 15:25-31}. Saul's repentance was not followed by a change in attitude. Repentance without remorse lasts no longer than a breath mint.

And so, *"Now the Spirit of the LORD had departed from Saul..."* {1 Sam 16:14 NIV}

Because of Saul's disobedience and his lack of genuine repentance the Lord withdrew His Spirit from Him. The Bible goes on to say that Saul was tormented by an evil spirit. In contrast, David's story was much different:

David's prayer to the Lord. He Repents.

"Have mercy on me, O God, according to your unfailing love, according to your great compassion blot out my transgressions. Wash away all my iniquity and cleanse me from my sin. For I know my transgressions, and my sin is always before me. Against you, you only, have I sinned and done what is evil in your sight, so you are right in your verdict and justified when you judge. Surely, I was sinful at birth, sinful from the time my mother conceived me. Yet you desired faithfulness even in the womb; you taught me wisdom in that secret place. Cleanse me with hyssop, and I will be clean; wash me, and I will be whiter than snow. Let me hear joy and gladness; let the bones you have crushed rejoice. Hide your face from my sins and blot out all my iniquity.Create in me a pure heart, O God, and renew a steadfast spirit within me.Do not cast me from your presence or take your Holy Spirit from me. Restore to me the joy of your salvation and grant me a willing spirit, to sustain

me. Then I will teach transgressors your ways so that sinners will turn back to you. Deliver me from the guilt of bloodshed, O God, you who are God my Savior, and my tongue will sing of your righteousness. Open my lips, Lord, and my mouth will declare your praise. You do not delight in sacrifice, or I would bring it; you do not take pleasure in burnt offerings. My sacrifice, O God, is a broken spirit; a broken and contrite heart you, God, will not despise. {Psalm 51 NIV}

David's life is a telling example of what we all know. Believers may sin. However, just because someone sins or even returns to their former sinful nature for a season, it does not always mean that they never experienced genuine repentance. Further, it does not mean they never received salvation at an earlier time. The difference between David and Saul was in the attitude of their hearts. They both had a relationship with God, but only David loved the Lord with all of his heart, soul and mind and therefore, he stayed in an active and on-going relationship with God. But, Saul was severed from God because of his lack of genuine repentance and his continued disobedience. It is the same for us. The attitude of the heart and the sincerity of our repentance are what matter most when we are confronted with or convicted by sin.

*"I am coming soon. **Hold on to what you have so that no one will take your crown.**"* {Rev 3:11 NIV}

In other words, Don't Die in the Pew.

CHAPTER TEN

Narrow Gate or Broad Way

Many professing Christians haven't picked up a Bible in years. Instead, they rely on the Church to feed them spiritually. But, if the Church is tiptoeing through the Bible and staying in its comfort zones, there will be a lack of knowledge throughout the entire Church body. As a result, souls may be at risk. The Bible warns that in the last days, many churches will effectively throw the truth right out the window. We open ourselves to this possibility when we "go with the flow" and follow the parade. This kind of deception won't be noticeable because it will sound right.

We will all live somewhere in eternity. The most important question at hand is where we will end up. There are only two ways we can go. Our challenge is that there is an entrance on each path, and both of them have a marquee at the gate that says, "Heaven." But, only one of them actually leads there. Does anyone really think, "I don't care if I spend eternity in Hell?" The fundamental problem is that the path that leads to Hell will never look like Hell. The path to Hell has a lot of nice people on it too. They will assure you that God wants you to be happy, so it's ok to do whatever you want, as long as you believe in Jesus. There are so many people on this path that we may find ourselves questioning and even second-guessing God's Word. I mean, surely this many people could not be deceived, could they? How could this be? It happens because there is a master of deception who is on the prowl. He is the ultimate counterfeit. We can be confident that he will make the path to Hell look like the way to Heaven. The Old Testament tells us about a way that seems right, but its end is the way of death. Walking through the narrow gate is not following an easy religion. We know this because it is the difficult way, and Jesus said that only a few actually find it. The Lord promised that the Kingdom opens up to those who seek Him with all of their hearts. But, when we do find the truth and set out on the narrow path, it won't be easy. It's not easy to deny ourselves and take up our cross to follow Christ while we live in a culture that constantly affirms the opposite. It's not easy to reject our own desires and to turn from our sins. Humbling ourselves is hard and so is genuine repentance.

*"Enter through the narrow gate. For **wide is the gate and broad is the road that leads to destruction**, and **<u>many enter</u>** through it. But **small is the gate and narrow the road that leads to life, and <u>only a few find it</u>**."* {Matt 7:13-14 NIV}

It is interesting that the very last book of the New Testament states this, *"**Blessed are those who do His commandments, <u>that they may have the right</u>** to the tree of life, **<u>and may enter through the gates</u>** into the city... I, Jesus, have sent My angel to testify to you these things in the churches..."* {Rev 22:14;16}

There it is, in black and white. This verse gives us the key to the narrow path.

Pop Quiz: Who does it say will have the right to the tree of life and the right to enter through the gates?

Answer Key: "those who DO His commandments."

This narrow way is not easy. However, Broad Street is wide open. It's fun. By the world's standards, most of the people on the broad path are actually good people. But don't be deceived, the broad way is not just for atheists and unbelievers. On this broad path, there will likely be no mention or concern over sin or the need to ensure correct theology. There won't be an emphasis on God's requirements for righteous living. Broad Street is the place where everyone seeks to do what is right in his own eyes. It is a path of self-gratification for all who put "self" before God. How many professing Christians sit in churches on Sunday but spend their time during the week wandering Broad Street?

Sadly, most people don't seek to know God's will. Why? Well, it's pretty simple. First, of all, it's not easy. It requires effort. It requires picking up the Word of God. It requires a relationship with Him which will lead us away from a self-gratifying or pleasure-seeking lifestyle. It requires time... and more than an hour on Sunday. Most have no desire to honor God with their lives, and so they don't look for evidence of His care and direction in their life. Yet, they profess great love for Jesus with their lips and claim they belong to the Kingdom. However, what is even more disturbing is that one can maintain a sense of complacent safety within a number of today's churches. Like our society, many churches seek not to offend, even at the cost of compromising God's Word. Today's gospel of accommodation is salvation without self-denial. It is the path of least resistance. Today, the "saved" walk arm in arm with the world, and it is often hard to distinguish between the lifestyle of a professing believer and the unbeliever. Do you recall the Nicolaitans? You know the ones with the doctrine that the Lord said He "hated." They come to mind again in this discussion.

The grace of God has been twisted into a license for immorality, and the Lordship of Jesus is casually rejected. Today, many professing believers just "go along to get along." My pastor has a wise position on this topic. He says that if we fit in too well with society, we might want to examine ourselves spiritually. We shouldn't fit in. We should stand out. Why? Because we were not made for this world. And, as Christians, we are Holy, and the word Holy does not mean that we have been perfected, it simply means that we are dedicated and "set apart."

"...Don't you realize that friendship with the world makes you an enemy of God? I say it again: If you want to be a friend of the world, you make yourself an enemy of God. **Do you think the Scriptures have no meaning?** *They say that God is passionate that the spirit he has placed within us should be faithful to him."* {James 4:4-5 NLT}

While the narrow path is steep, the gate to Broad Street can be entered quite easily. There is no need for repentance or transformation. All you have to do is believe in Jesus. To enter, you won't even have to leave anything behind. Bring all of your baggage. There are no boundaries and no borders because we need to be tolerant, even compromising, so we can help people feel loved and accepted. There is room for immorality and the pursuit of worldly pleasures. There is even room for different theology. We don't want to offend anyone who might have diverse religious beliefs, do we? All is acceptable on Broad Street because where there is no vision or revelation of the law, the people are unrestrained. We are in a battle within our souls to release

182

our love of sin and pride. The narrow way is one that involves discipline and self-restraint. We might even suffer persecution. Jesus told us, "Don't be surprised if the world hates you because it hated me first." It is vitally important that we fully grasp the fact that we are following Jesus Christ and not a manual for a moral life.

The the sum total of the Christian faith is not the laws, principles, and guidance that we are instructed to obey. If we view the requirements outside the context of Christ, it will lead us, in error, down a path of legalism and self-righteousness. Due to the constructs of the Jewish religion of his time, the Apostle Paul continually ran up against those who touted legalism and self-righteousness as the only path to God. The religion of the Pharisees can be summed up in Luke 18:9. It says that they *"trusted in themselves that they were righteous,"* their hope depended entirely upon what they did. It depended on their works, alone.

Faith comes by hearing the message of Christ. It is by Christ, and through Him alone, that we enter through the narrow gate. The instructions given to us for righteous living are not the means by which we are justified and deemed righteous. Jesus said, *"You search the Scriptures because you think that in them you have eternal life; it is these that testify about Me, and you are unwilling to come to Me so that you may have life."* {John 5:39-40}

Jesus was warning those of His day that they could not find eternal life through a "code of conduct." Today, we seem to have gone to the opposite extreme, resulting in confusion within the Church, and in our faith.

A relationship with Jesus cannot be separated from the guidance and commands of Scripture, neither can the guidance and commands be separated from the act of establishing a relationship with Christ and exalting Him as Lord over our lives. A sincere attitude of repentance will compel us to respond to His grace and love with devotion and obedience. What do you think the Lord wants from us? Everything. That's all. *"Therefore, I urge you, brothers and sisters, **in view of God's mercy**, to **offer your bodies as a living sacrifice**, holy and pleasing to God—**this is your true and proper worship**. Do not conform to the pattern of this world, but be transformed by the renewing of your mind. Then you will be able to test and approve what God's will is—his good, pleasing and perfect will."* {Rom 12:1-2 NIV}

Jesus said that it is vain to call him Lord and not follow His instructions. As we walk in our faith each day and grow in spiritual knowledge, it is vital that we humbly examine our lives on a continual basis and promptly make changes if our life and actions don't line up with the teachings of Christ. Charles Spurgeon said, "You and your sins must separate, or you and your God cannot come together." Many churches today have become "seeker friendly." The result is evident in the carefully crafted messages that won't offend anyone. Did the Lord instruct us to water down the gospel at any point? The reality is that the Bible will offend. But, the knowledge gained from His Word will also save souls. If we don't seek God and pursue a love relationship by getting to know Him through the Bible, we probably won't see much transformation, if any. *"Seek the LORD while He may be found, Call upon Him while He is near."* {Isaiah 55:6 NIV}

"But you do not believe, because you are not of My sheep, as I said to you. My sheep hear My voice, and I know them, and they follow Me. And I give them eternal life, and they shall

never perish; neither shall anyone snatch them out of My hand. My Father, who has given them to Me, is greater than all; and no one is able to snatch them out of My Father's hand." {John 10:26-29}

Did this verse say anything about being impossible for a "sheep" to lose his place in the Shepherd's pen? No, it absolutely does not! It is telling us that the Father and the Son are stronger than anyone who might attempt to "snatch" the believer from either of their hands. But, a sheep can always wander off and get lost. This Scripture is not an unconditional promise for eternal salvation, it is a promise of protection. It demonstrates the power of God against external forces.

Jesus said that if you belong to Him, you will hear His voice. "My sheep hear My voice" Do you have any doubt about your relationship with Jesus? Do you hear His voice? Once we sincerely ask the Lord into our lives, the Holy Spirit comes to live inside of us. It is the same Spirit of the Living God that indwelt Jesus while He was on the earth. When Jesus returned to heaven, the Holy Spirit was sent to us as a comforter. He will teach, guide, and protect us. He will open our eyes to the truth. He is God! He manifests Himself in different ways to each of us. He may speak through the Bible. Your time in His Word may provide revelation from His Spirit. He may speak through prayer. You may hear a word from God in your spirit. He may speak to us through the Church. A pastor's sermon may strike a chord. He may speak through other believers. People who God places in our lives may give us confirmation. Most importantly, we should always confirm that what people speak to us in "faith," is in alignment with the Bible and the character of Christ. The Bible becomes our filter, and if we are reading the Word of God, we will begin to understand His nature, His attributes and His heart.

If you're not sure that you've ever heard from God, don't dismiss that question. We all need to be sure we belong to Him. We are advised to test ourselves and be sure we are in the faith. If you are unsure, stop now, repent and confess from your heart. Ask Jesus to forgive you. Ask Him to change you into the person He wants you to be. Get into His Word daily and let the Holy Spirit teach you. By the power of Christ living in you, He will enable you to stop doing the things that are in opposition to His instructions.

A prayer from your heart will be sufficient and welcomed by Him. Just confess with your mouth and believe in your heart that Jesus is the son of God who died for your sins, then rose from the dead so that you might have eternal life. Acknowledge Him as Lord and Repent! Then, be diligent to seek Him and read the Bible. *"You will seek me and find me when you seek me with all your heart."* {Jer 29:13 NIV}

The Lord is longsuffering, which means He is patient. He has delayed His coming so that people will come to repentance.

"Who hindered you from obeying the truth? This persuasion does not come from Him who calls you... but he who troubles you shall bear his judgment, whoever he is." {Gal 5:7-8,10}

He requires to be on the throne in our life. If you are reading this and thinking, "but that refers to works." Yes, it does! And, the Bible says that faith without works is dead. It is foolish to skip over every other verse that does not speak about the free gift of grace. It is by grace alone that we are able to stand, and it is then because of grace that we are called to walk in the newness of life and put off our former ways. Period. In all likelihood, after receiving God's grace, we will sin again. The Lord knew we were not able to do it on our own, so He gave us a helper and He put His Holy Spirit within us.

The more we mature in our understanding and our knowledge of Christ, the more we will willfully and joyfully live in the Spirit and choose to die to the desires of our flesh.

"And those who are Christ's have crucified the flesh with its passions and desires." {Gal 5:24}

We can be renewed and equipped each day, and this happens as we spend time with the Lord. In doing so, we can overcome the temptations of the world and bring glory to our Father in heaven by remaining faithful to the Lord throughout our day. As we spend time in His Word, keep in mind that He promised to give us wisdom to discern things that are hard to understand. *"If any of you lacks wisdom, you should ask God, who gives generously to all without finding fault, and it will be given to you"* {James 1:5}

To avoid confusion, I'd like to clarify something. We are not in and then suddenly out of fellowship with the Lord because we sin. When we have received grace, we will not be condemned by the law **if** we are walking according to the Spirit (in an active relationship with Christ) and not the flesh. Practically speaking, this means that we are standing on His promises, and we are remaining in Him by the power of the Spirit and through the truth in His Word. We should be abiding in Him each and every day by spending quality time in some way that honors Him. This may be a time of thoughtful and sincere prayer. It might be time spent studying and reading His Word or in fellowship with other believers. You may spend time praising the Lord or worshipping from the heart. The Bible says we enter into his courts with praise. You may want to journal your thoughts or prayers in a letter to the Lord. There is one thing that is certain, your time spent with Him must be intentional.

"And a highway will be there; it will be called the Way of Holiness; it will be for those who walk on that Way. The unclean will not journey on it; wicked fools will not go about on it. {Isa 35:8 NIV}

One of the most profound points I have ever heard is this: even Satan and his demons believe in God. They believe that Jesus is the son of God and that He came to earth to die on the cross to save us from our sins. Knowledge does not equate to a relationship. I know all about the President of the United States, but he doesn't know me. We have no relationship, though he does represent and protect me as a citizen of the United States. I see him on television. I may know parts of his personal history. Yet, if I show up at the White House and ask to come in and stay a while, I am certain to be turned away. If I have no personal relationship with Christ, I will get a similar reply when I approach His throne, "depart from me, I do not know you." Without personal time together, it is impossible to know someone. You only know about them.

*"Therefore, since Christ suffered in his body, **arm yourselves also with the same attitude**, because whoever suffers in the body is **done with sin**. As a result, they **do not live the rest of their earthly lives for evil human desires, but rather for the will of God.** For you have spent enough time in the past doing what pagans choose to do— living in debauchery, lust, drunkenness, orgies, carousing and detestable idolatry. They are surprised that you do not join them in their reckless, wild living, and they heap abuse on you. But they will have to give account to him who is*

ready to judge the living and the dead. For this is the reason, the gospel was preached even to those who are now dead, so that they might be judged according to human standards in regard to the body but live according to God in regard to the spirit. The end of all things is near. Therefore, be alert and of sober mind so that you may pray. Above all, love each other deeply, because love covers over a multitude of sins. Offer hospitality to one another without grumbling. Each of you should use whatever gift you have received to serve others, as faithful stewards of God's grace in its various forms. If anyone speaks, they should do so as one who speaks the very words of God. If anyone serves, they should do so with the strength God provides, so that in all things God may be praised through Jesus Christ. To him be the glory and the power for ever and ever. Amen." {1 Peter 4:1-11 NIV}

"The one who does what is sinful is of the devil, because the devil has been sinning from the beginning. The reason the Son of God appeared was to destroy the devil's work. No one who is born of God will continue to sin, because God's seed remains in them; they cannot go on sinning, because they have been born of God. ***This is how we know who the children of God are and who the children of the devil are:*** *Anyone who does not do what is right is not God's child, nor is anyone who does not love their brother and sister."* {John 3:8-10}

CHAPTER ELEVEN

Examining the Parables

The Prodigal Son

Let's consider the parable of the prodigal son. There are so many lessons in this story. The child who will become the prodigal, is living in his father's house. The father represents God. The son leaves his father's home and goes to a faraway country. While there, he wastes all of his wealth and possessions in sinful living. Then, the Bible says, *"...he came to himself,"* which we can obviously take to mean that he came to his senses. The son decided to repent and return to his father. *"And the son said to him, 'Father, I have sinned against heaven and in your sight, and am no longer worthy to be called your son."* The father says, *"For this, my son **was dead**, and is **alive again**; he was lost and is found."*

Biblically speaking, to be dead is to be unsaved, and to be alive is to be saved. *"You were at one time spiritually dead because of your sins..."* {Col 2:13}

Don't miss the fact that the father says that his son is alive "again." In other words, at the beginning of the parable, the son was alive, or saved, when he was in his father's house. He was "dead," or unsaved after he willfully chose to leave his father's house to live his life on his own terms. When he returned to his father's home, he was repentant and sorrowful over his disobedience and his sin. As a result, the story tells us that he was considered to be "alive again."

Alive, dead, alive again. Saved, unsaved, saved again.

This parable is an excellent example of what the Bible tells us about our eternal security. Until we draw our last breath, there is hope. We are sealed by the Holy Spirit for the day of redemption, but the names written on the scroll in the Lamb's Book of Life will not be opened until the day of judgment. In the book of Revelation, the Lord says, *"**He who overcomes** shall be clothed in white garments, and I will not **blot out his name from the Book of Life**, but I will confess his name before My Father and before His angels."* {Rev 3:5}

If we are still on this earth, we can turn our hearts back towards home and away from our willful disobedience. When we do, our Father will celebrate our return and welcome us back into His presence, without condemnation. His sacrifice will pay the penalty each and every time we truly repent, as long as we remain in fellowship with Him. This is the process of "being" sanctified. Think about the Israelites. For as many times as they forsook the Lord when they were wandering in the desert and throughout history, God continued to tell them to repent. It is not different for us. We are consistently told throughout the New Testament to repent, to overcome and to remain steadfast to the end.

"…if My people who are called by My name will humble themselves, and pray and seek My face, and turn from their wicked ways, then I will hear from heaven, and will forgive their sin and heal their land." {2 Chronicles 7:14 NIV}

Jesus Tells the Parable of the Sower

*"Then he told them many things in parables, saying: "A farmer went out to sow his seed. As he was scattering the seed, some fell along the path, and the birds came and ate it up. Some fell on rocky places, where it did not have much soil. It sprang up quickly, because the soil was shallow. But when the sun came up, the plants were scorched, and they withered because they had no root. Other seed fell among thorns, which grew up and choked the plants. Still other seed fell on good soil, where it produced a crop—a hundred, sixty or thirty times what was sown. Whoever has ears, let them hear." The disciples came to him and asked, "Why do you speak to the people in parables?" He replied, "Because the knowledge of the secrets of the kingdom of heaven has been given to you, but not to them. Whoever has will be given more, and they will have an abundance. Whoever does not have, even what they have will be taken from them. **This is why I speak to them in parables: Though seeing, they do not see; though hearing, they do not hear or understand.***" {Matt 13:3-13 NIV}*

There is a recurring theme throughout many of Christ's parables. In the parable of the sower, the talents, the ten virgins, and the tree known by its fruit, He offers a consistent message. He gives a warning to believers. That is powerful!! It is imperative, and it should encourage us to seek spiritual discernment.

Jesus Explains the Parable of the Sower

As you read the explanation Jesus gave for the parable, notice that a plant sprouts or starts to grow in three of the four scenarios, but only one of them survives to the end.

"Therefore, hear the parable of the sower: "When anyone **hears the word** *of the kingdom* **and does not understand it,** *then the wicked one comes and snatches away what was sown in his heart. This is he who received* **seed by the wayside.** *But he who received the seed on stony places, this is he who* **hears the word** *and* **immediately receives it with joy;** *yet he has no root in himself* **but endures only for a while.** *For when tribulation or* **persecution arises because of the word,** *immediately* **he stumbles.** *Now he who received seed among the thorns is he who* **hears the word, and the cares of this world and the deceitfulness of riches choke the word,** *and* **he becomes unfruitful.** *But he who received seed on the good ground is he who* **hears the word and understands it, who indeed bears fruit and produces:** *some a hundredfold, some sixty, some thirty."* {Matt 13:18-23}

The condition of your heart will determine your response to God's Word. If your heart is hardened by bitterness, un-forgiveness, and sin, then it will be stony and unreceptive to any message from the Lord. The one who hears the Word and immediately "receives it with joy" is the one who accepted Christ in their heart, but their faith had little to no root. Why? Because the heart was not penetrated with Godly sorrow which leads to true repentance. He explains that these people endure for a while, until the "Christian thing" gets a little tough. They remain until they are faced with persecution "because of the Word." When these things happen, it gets harder to be "all-in." When the Bible refers to the one who allows the Word to get "choked out," it implies that the Word was in his heart at some point, but the pursuits and pleasures of this life were more important. They prevented God's Word from sinking in and producing righteousness. Another clue is that he becomes unfruitful, which is again, an implication that he had previously been fruitful. The only one on good soil was the one who heard the Word,

194

understood it and then bore fruit. I believe Jesus is giving us an example of various Christians who are in different stages of life and faith. They hear and receive the Word, but they don't understand it. Therefore, they don't produce fruit. The fruit that Jesus is talking about in this parable is fruit that helps win "souls" for the Kingdom. He wants us to preserve souls and to multiply the Kingdom. We are all called to be ambassadors for Christ.

There are some who teach that the three hearers described in this parable, the ones who don't make it to the end, are not actually falling away. Rather, they suggest that those who fell away were probably never truly saved in the first place. I respectfully disagree.

During a conversation with a friend of mine, she shared that she sincerely believed in her heart and professed Jesus as Lord in her mid-twenties. She explained that afterwards, she went to church and she even felt God leading her at times, but she continued to live an unchanged life. Years later, she realized that she did not actually have a genuine relationship with Christ. In her mid-forties, she said she heard God speak to her, and it impacted her in such a way that she began to actively and intentionally pursue Him. As a result of the true transformation in her forties, she discussed it with her pastor, and he convinced her that she was probably not genuinely saved beforehand. I asked her, "when you originally professed your faith in Jesus and believed on Him as Lord for the first time in your twenties, did you mean it? She said, "Yes, she did." But, she explained that she did not pursue learning more, so she didn't think she grew as a Christian. I told her that I believe that she became a Christian in the first moment that she professed her faith and believed in her heart, if in fact, those two things were true. The Bible says, *that if you confess with your mouth the Lord*

195

*Jesus and believe in your heart that God has raised Him from the dead, **you will be saved.**"* {Rom 10:9}

According to the true Word of God, it happens in that moment. But, what happens concerning our spiritual growth after that is, at least in part, based on our own decisions. It is similar to what the Lord is doing with Israel. He said that He is not restoring them for their sake, He is doing it for the sake of His Holy Name. He is keeping His Word. What He has promised that will He do. End of Story.

To say that someone who has believed in their heart (this is the primary component) and professed with their mouth that Jesus is Lord and is still not truly saved, is actually saying that there is more required for justification in Christ. This is biblically untrue. It is also asserting that we cannot take Romans 10:9 literally. That is a lie. God's Word is absolute truth. You WILL be saved when you profess with your mouth and believe in your heart that Jesus is Lord and Savior. God keeps His Word! The journey requires endurance and a heart that is intentional towards walking with the King of Kings as Lord over our life. Jesus promised us that "we will" find Him when we seek Him with all of our heart. In the great commission, Jesus instructed us to fish for people and then teach new Christians all He has commanded them "to do." Unfortunately, and all too often, new Christians sometimes lack spiritual guidance and need a mature Christian friend or mentor to help them in the way they should go. This is the piece that my friend was missing. But, how faithful is our God? Even when we do not pursue Him, He still pursues us.

Before Jesus ascended, He told the disciples to wait for the promise of the Holy Spirit. He said that the Holy Spirit would not come until He had departed.

- *"But you will receive power* when the Holy Spirit has come upon you; and *you will be my witnesses* in Jerusalem, and in all Judea and Samaria, and to the end of the earth." {Acts 1:8 NIV}

- *"We are therefore Christ's ambassadors, as though God were making his appeal through us.* We implore you on Christ's behalf: Be reconciled to God." {2 Cor 5:20 NIV}

Beware of the Leaven of the Pharisees

*Then **Jesus said to them, "Take heed and beware of the leaven of the Pharisees** and the Sadducees." And they reasoned among themselves, saying, "It is because we have taken no bread." But Jesus, being aware of it, said to them, "O you of little faith, why do you reason among yourselves because you have brought no bread? ...**How is it you do not understand that I did not speak to you concerning bread?** --but to beware of the leaven of the Pharisees and Sadducees." Then they understood that **He did not tell them to beware of the leaven of bread, but of the doctrine of the Pharisees** and Sadducees.* {Matt 16:6-8, 10-12}

In the book of Mark, Jesus also cautioned them to beware of the Leaven of Herod too. Jesus tells us what He meant. *"He began to say to His disciples first of all, "Beware of the leaven of the Pharisees, **which is hypocrisy.**"* {Luke 12:1} "Hypocrite" comes from the Greek word hupokrites and refers to someone who is acting or pretending. However, the Leaven of the Pharisees is more than hypocrisy. *"...He did not tell them to beware of the leaven of bread, but of **the doctrine** of the Pharisees and*

Sadducees." {Matt 16:12} Jesus saw how both parties were corrupting God's message.

Today, there are many ministers who dilute the message of repentance for the approval of modern-day audiences. "Preaching" has become an art, which is often supplemented by glitzy multi-media presentations. While there is nothing wrong with this, listeners can become more enamored with the messenger and the experience, rather than the truth from God's Word. The fermentation of yeast is the secret ingredient to making bread rise. It only takes a small amount added to bread dough to have its full effect. Jesus is saying that the Pharisees and Sadducees are taking something that is good and useful, and they are making it useless by adding just a little bit of their own spin. The more we add to biblical messages, the more we actually detract from the original intent of Scripture. The more we water down the message of the gospel to appeal to what "itching ears want to hear," the greater the impurity grows. Jesus warned us to watch out for those who are altering His message.

Before his conversion, Paul had been a Pharisee; therefore, he could recognize the connection between leaven and malicious intent. Paul said, *"Therefore let us keep the Festival, not with old bread leavened with malice and wickedness, but with the unleavened bread of sincerity and truth."* {1 Cor 5:8 NIV} Let's be on guard against Leaven. If what we hear does not line up with the gospel of truth, we need to recognize it and reject it. *"For such people are false apostles, deceitful workers, masquerading as apostles of Christ. And no wonder, for Satan himself masquerades as an angel of light. It is not surprising, then, if his servants also masquerade as servants of righteousness. Their end will be what their actions deserve."* {2 Cor 11:13-15 NIV}

I don't believe that everyone who misinterprets the Bible, is attempting to intentionally sabotage the Church. I think that what is happening is more subtle. Most often, the battlefield the enemy uses is in our own mind. While the devil may not be able to read our mind, he can absolutely influence our thoughts. Sound a little far-fetched? Well, just in case you're not sure you believe that, let's go to the Bible. *"The evening meal was in progress, and* **the devil had already put into the heart of** *Judas Iscariot, Simon's son,* **that he should betray Jesus."** {John 13:2}

We should seek to discern who is speaking to us. *"Therefore, submit to God. Resist the devil, and he will flee from you."* {James 4:7}

If you are teaching God's word, proceed with caution!

- *"Not many of you should become teachers, my fellow believers, because you know that we who teach will be judged more strictly."* {James 3:1 NIV}

- *"Be diligent to present yourself approved to God, a worker who does not need to be ashamed,* **rightly dividing the word of truth."** {2 Tim 2:15}

- *"He must hold firm to the trustworthy word as taught, so that he may be able to give instruction in* **sound doctrine** *and also to* **rebuke those who contradict it."** {Titus 1:9}

False doctrine comes in many deceiving forms. When a distortion of the truth is presented as doctrine, it will unduly influence the opinions and philosophies of men, and ultimately, it will pervert the true gospel.

A Faithful and Wise Servant

"Who then is the faithful and wise servant, **whom the master has put in charge of the servants in his household** *to give them their food at the proper time? It will be good for that servant whose master finds him doing so when he returns. Truly I tell you, he will put him in charge of all his possessions.* **But suppose that servant is wicked and says to himself, 'My master is staying away a long time,'** *and he then begins to beat his fellow servants and to eat and drink with drunkards. The master of that servant will come on a day when he does not expect him and at an hour he is not aware of.* **He will cut him to pieces and assign him a place with the hypocrites,** *where there will be weeping and gnashing of teeth."* {Matt 24:45-51 NIV}

In each reference, both the good and evil are the master's servants, which infers that they both belong to him. When Jesus is referring to the master "coming" for them, it is an illustration of Christ returning for the people of Israel and the Church, a promise which is given to His children. But, the servant who will be blessed is the one He finds "doing" what He instructed him to do.

Jesus tells us, this evil servant decided to live life his own way. One might presume that he felt he was safe because of the grace of his Master. He was too busy to make time for God, but he had time for his friends and enjoying the pleasures of life. The master catches him by surprise, and he moved him to a place with the hypocrites! We don't have to be a genius to follow the logic that if he was appointing him with the hypocrites, then at an earlier point, he had not been with the hypocrites. He had an opportunity to follow the master's plan, but instead, he chose to enjoy his life on the Broad Way.

Whether you like tests or not, every person who has ever lived will take a final exam. This exam is not going to measure how many books of the Bible we can recite. I feel relatively confident that we will not need to answer any Bible trivia. Instead, our lives are going to be examined. We will be measured against God's Word, and this will determine the final location of our eternal home.

Jesus said, *"the word that I have spoken will judge him in the last day"* {John 12:48}.

God will judge us through our relationship with Christ. I have to imagine that the first questions will be, "Who has Jesus been to you? Who did you tell?" God will bring all of our works into judgment including every secret thing good or evil. Nothing will remain as secret. *"The time is coming when everything that is covered up will be revealed, and all that is secret will be made known to all. Whatever you have said in the dark will be heard in the light, and what you have whispered behind closed doors will be shouted from the housetops for all to hear!"* {Luke 12:2-3 NLT}

According to the Bible, there will be three categories against which we will be judged. The Bible also teaches us that both the living and the dead, as well as the saved and the unsaved, must give an account to Christ.

1) Words Spoken

> *"But I say to you that for **every idle word** men may speak, they will give account of it in the day of judgment. For by your words you will be justified, and by your words, you will be condemned."* {Matt 12:36-37}

201

2) Our Actions

> *"For we must **all appear** before the judgment seat of Christ, that each one may receive the things done in the body, according to what he has done, whether good or bad."* {2 Cor 5:10}

3) Our Motives (the condition of our heart)

> *"So don't make judgments about anyone ahead of time—before the Lord returns. **For he will bring our darkest secrets to light and will reveal our private motives.** Then God will give to each one whatever praise is due."* {1 Cor 4:5 NLT}

We all struggle, and we all sin. The real question is whether we genuinely desire to become closer to God. Do we want to fellowship with Him? If we are sincere and trying to live for God, then our actions will naturally follow the desire. We will begin to trust God's promises and go to Him in prayer as a regular part of our daily life. When we become aware of our sins, a sincere desire to grow in Christ will prompt us to confess and to turn away from them. A heart that is anchored in Christ will desire to read and study God's Word. Knowing that Christ exists and being close to Him are very different. The Holy Spirit will soften our hearts, and we will actually enjoy being around His people. We will want to worship with others, not out of obligation, but out of the attitude of a transformed heart. We will sense a desire in our Spirit to remove gossip, jealousy, greed, lust, dishonesty, hatred and anger from our lives. We will be enabled to overcome these things by the power of the Holy Spirit that is living within us.

Luke's Account of the Faithful and Evil Servant

*Peter asked, "**Lord, are you telling this parable to us, or to everyone?**" The Lord answered, "Who then is the faithful and wise manager, whom the master puts in charge of his servants to give them their food allowance at the proper time? **It will be good for that servant whom the master finds doing so when he returns.** Truly I tell you, he will put him in charge of all his possessions. **But suppose the servant says to himself, 'My master is taking a long time in coming,'** and he then begins to beat the other servants, both men and women, and to eat and drink and get drunk. The master of that servant will come on a day when he does not expect him and at an hour he is not aware of. **He will cut him to pieces and assign him a place with the unbelievers.**"* {Luke 12:41-46 NIV}

Throughout this story, Jesus is referring to the same person who can choose a path: path A or path B. The Scriptures teach us that until a sinner has repented and called on Jesus, they are estranged from the Lord, and they do not belong to Him. He elaborates that the servant is Blessed "if" he is doing the will of the Father when Christ returns. However, if that same servant thinks to himself that the master is delayed, and then while waiting, willfully gives in to his own desires and returns to a sinful life, that servant will find himself in deep trouble when he is caught by surprise.

There is a crucial word in this verse, and it is the word "unbelievers." The master will place him among the "unbelievers." I really don't know how much more clearly stated this could be. From this parable, we can conclude that Christ is describing someone with whom He was in a relationship. But ultimately, He assigned this person to a place with the unbelievers as a result of willful disobedience.

10 Virgins

"Then the kingdom of heaven shall be likened to ten virgins who took their lamps and went out to meet the bridegroom. Now five of them were wise, and five were foolish. Those who were foolish took their lamps and took no oil with them, but the wise took oil in their vessels with their lamps. But while the bridegroom was delayed, they all slumbered and slept. And at midnight a cry was heard: 'Behold, the bridegroom is coming; go out to meet him! Then all those virgins arose and trimmed their lamps. And the foolish said to the wise, 'Give us some of your oil, for our lamps are going out.' But the wise answered, saying, 'No, lest there should not be enough for us and you; but go rather to those who sell, and buy for yourselves.' And while they went to buy, the bridegroom came, **and those who were ready** *went in with him to* **the wedding; and** **the door was shut***. Afterward, the* **other virgins came** *also, saying, 'Lord, Lord, open to us!' But he answered and said, '***Assuredly, I say to you, I do not know you.***"* {Matt 25:1-12}

In earlier chapters, we have already confirmed:

- God describes Himself as the husband of Israel, {Isa 54:4-6; Hosea 2:19}

- Jesus is described as the bridegroom of Israel and the Church. {John 3:27-30; Matt 9:15}

- Israel and the Church [which has been grafted in] are described as the Bride of Christ {Eph 5:25-32}.

I believe the oil in this passage is referring to the Word of God. The fact that all 10 people are virgins implies that they all appear pure on the outside. They are essentially all declaring the same thing, and they believe themselves to be Christians. They each take their lamp, which represents their bodies, and they go out to meet Christ, the bridegroom. Five were wise, and five were foolish. The foolish did not put lamp oil in their lamps. Meaning, that they did not seek truth for themselves in Scripture. They may have gone to church and just listened to sermons, but they never verified if what they were being told was the truth from God's Word. The lamp oil is the Word of God. As a result, the truth didn't get planted in their hearts. The wise took oil in their vessels. They clung to the truth in their Bible's and received discernment from the Holy Spirit. As a result, the Spirit began to enable them to live out the truths they were learning and caused them to be prepared and "fitted" at all times. But, the bridegroom did not hurry. He was delayed, and so they all slept and just went about their lives. A midnight cry was heard. He is Coming – Come to Meet Him! The foolish were surprised and scurried around because they didn't actually expect Him. They had been told He was coming, but they didn't take it seriously. They hadn't prepared themselves by studying the Word, and they had not allowed the Spirit to transform them. So, they continued living life their own way, for themselves. They asked for the wise to help them, but the wise told them to go and study for themselves. And while they hurried to fill their lamps, the bridegroom came, and when He came, He took the ones who were ready. Those were the ones who sought Him continually and who had remained in fellowship with Christ, the ones who endured. They were bearing fruit. They went in, and He shut the door. Afterward, the other virgins who are symbolic of Christians who had also professed faith in Jesus, they came too, and they were shocked. After all, they went to Church, and they even believed in Him. They listened to the sermons and they were in the pews on Sunday. But, He answered, "I do not know you."

Jesus said that there will be a lot of these types of people. *"Many will say to Me in that day, 'Lord, Lord, have we not prophesied in Your name, cast out demons in Your name, and done many wonders in Your name?' And then I will declare to them, 'I never knew you; depart from Me, you who practice lawlessness!"* {Matt 7:22-23}

This verse refers to someone who was engaged in spiritual warfare and actually cast out demons. This sounds like a life that had been devoted to the cause of Christ. These do not sound like the pleas of a superficial Christian, and yet, Jesus said "many" will believe they were on their way to heaven and will be shocked to find out that the door will not be opened. How could this happen? Perhaps they were devoted to the cause but not to an authentic relationship with Christ. To the recipient, these will be the most terrifying words ever spoken by Jesus, "I do not know you." Keep in mind how He identified them as "you who practice lawlessness." This will be a devastating moment for those who profess faith but who do not truly possess eternal life.

Lord, help us to see. Open our ears. Deliver us from evil. Father, I pray that you will give us wisdom and discernment in the midst of a wicked and self-gratifying generation. I pray that by your Holy Spirit, our hearts will be stirred and that we will be transformed by the renewing of our minds. Teach us your ways, God. Set our feet on paths of righteousness. Help us to understand saving grace and stir us to always be a repentant people full of love, mercy, and compassion. Give us resolve to stand boldly on the truths of your Word and to proclaim the gospel. Help us to remain in you. Strengthen and equip us each day. You are a good, good Father! In the mighty and all-powerful name of our Savior Jesus Christ, Amen!

A Man Traveling to a Far Country

"For the kingdom of heaven is like a man traveling to a far country, **who called** **his own** **servants** *and delivered his goods to them. And to one he gave five talents, to another two, and to another one, to each according to his own ability; and immediately he went on a journey._Then he who had received the five talents went and traded with them and made another five talents._And likewise, he who had received two gained two more also._But he who had received one went and dug in the ground and hid his lord's money._After a long time, the lord of those servants came and settled accounts with them._So, he who had received five talents came and brought five other talents, saying, 'Lord, you delivered to me five talents; look, I have gained five more talents besides them.' His lord said to him, 'Well done, good and faithful servant; you were faithful over a few things, I will make you ruler over many things. Enter into the joy of your lord. He also who had received two talents came and said, 'Lord, you delivered to me two talents; look, I have gained two more talents besides them. His lord said to him, 'Well done, good and faithful servant; you have been faithful over a few things, I will make you ruler over many things. Enter into the joy of your lord.' Then he who had received the one talent came and said, 'Lord, I knew you to be a hard man, reaping where you have not sown, and gathering where you have not scattered seed. And* **I was afraid** *and went* **and hid your talent in the ground**. *Look, there you have what is yours.' But his lord answered and said to him,* **'You wicked and lazy servant**, *you knew that I reap where I have not sown and gather where I have not scattered seed. So, you ought to have deposited my money with the bankers, and at my coming, I would have received back my own with interest. Therefore, take the talent from him, and give it to him who has ten talents. For to everyone who has, more will be given, and he will have abundance; but from him who does not have,* even what he *has will be taken away. And* **cast the**

unprofitable <u>servant</u> into the outer darkness. There will be weeping and gnashing of teeth." {Matt 25:14-30}

We will be without excuse. In the Word of God, Jesus is giving a warning to Christians, or people that profess to be. The man traveling away to a far country for a while is Christ, and the far country is heaven, where Jesus resides at the right hand of the Father. He says, the man traveling who called **his own servants** (this is key). The goods he delivered are the precious treasure of divine truths in the Word of God and gifts to preach it. The critical point is this: All the servants belonged to the Master. The servant that buried his talent because of fear, produced nothing! The Lord called him wicked and lazy. He explains that this servant could have deposited his money in the bank, meaning that he could have used his life to deposit the Word into other souls. If he had, then at "His Return," this servant would have received the talent back, and with interest. The "interest" is souls preserved, which glorifies the Father and increases the Kingdom. Jesus made it clear what happens to the unprofitable (or for our purposes, the unfruitful) servant whose end will be outer darkness. The Bible refers to outer darkness as "Hell." I don't know about you, but it sounds like bearing fruit is pretty important.

Fig Tree in His Vineyard Not Bearing Fruit

*Then he told this parable: "A man had a fig tree growing in his vineyard, and **he went to look for fruit on it but did not find any.** So he said to the man who took care of the vineyard, 'For three years now I've been coming to look for fruit on this fig tree and haven't found any. **Cut it down!** Why should it use up the soil?' 'Sir,' the man replied, 'leave it alone for one more year, and I'll dig around it and fertilize it. **If it bears fruit next year, fine! If not, then cut it down.'"** {Luke 13:6-9 NIV}

Here is what we can glean from scripture: *"I am the true vine, and my Father is the vinedresser."* {John 15:1}

Webster's Dictionary says that a vinedresser is "a person who cultivates and prunes grapevines." The good news is that God is merciful, and He is willing to forgive. However, the sterner portion of this parable is illustrating that even God's patient mercy has limits. In this example, we are shown that if the tree has stopped producing fruit for a while, then something needs to change. The tree is not dead or incapable of producing fruit. The tree hasn't had the proper care and nourishment, and it's just there, passing the time. The tree is like many people in our society. They wander around every day, alive and breathing, but they live their lives aimlessly, not really growing or going anywhere... not bearing fruit.

CHAPTER TWELVE

The Conclusion of the Matter

When we have a problem with God's Word, assuredly the problem is in our understanding of His Word. It is never a problem WITH His Word. We need a spirit of humility as we read and interpret the Bible. When our heart is authentic, and when we are genuinely seeking the Lord, we will be in the position to gain wisdom and receive discernment. The Lord exalts the humble and brings down the prideful.

"If any of you lacks wisdom, you should ask God, who gives generously to all without finding fault, and it will be given to you. But when you ask, you must believe and not doubt, because the one who doubts is like a wave of the sea, blown and tossed by the wind. That person should not expect to receive anything from the Lord. Such a person is double-minded and unstable in all they do." {James 1:5-9 NIV}

*"Don't let anyone capture you with empty philosophies and **high-sounding nonsense that come from human thinking** and from the spiritual powers of this world, rather than from Christ."* {Col 2:8 NLT}

"For <u>you have need</u> of endurance, so that <u>after you have</u> <u>done the will of God</u>, <u>you may</u> receive the promise: For yet a little while, And He who is coming will come and will not tarry. Now the just shall live by faith; <u>But if anyone</u> <u>draws back</u>, My soul has no pleasure in him." {Hebrews 10:36-38}

I may be preaching to the choir, but there is a recurring theme that is worthy of acknowledgement. We miss so much when we just gloss over Scriptures like this one. So often, we quickly move on to the next verse, you know, the one that speaks only of the love of God. Don't get me wrong, I love warm and fuzzy verses too. They give me a great deal of comfort. However, if grace through faith is the only requirement for eternal life, then why is it written that "we have need" of endurance, so that "after we have done the will of God," "we may" receive the promise. What do we do with this verse?

Within the pages of the Bible we have all of the wisdom needed to navigate perfectly within every area of our lives. If we want our lives to align with what pleases the Lord, we need to go to His Word. His guidance is not meant to be a burden or to make our lives dull. Everything He has told us is for our good, it is to protect us from the harm that comes from sin. I want to recognize the guidance of the Holy Spirit as He works to transform me. If I sense Him prompting me to stop watching television shows that don't espouse the values we represent, I want to turn off the TV. For many of us, He may reveal in our heart that we need to find a new set of friends. The Bible says, *"Walk with the wise and become wise, for a companion of fools suffers harm."* {Prov 13:20} Are we hanging around the type of people that inspire us to become more like Christ, or do our friends influence us in a way that is anchored in

212

self-indulgence, gossip and worldly desires? We may need to get up earlier each day, so we'll have time to read the Bible before work. Regardless of what transformation looks like for each of us personally, if we are truly following Christ, there will be a transformation in our lives. He will teach us and lead us in His ways. But, as we have established, endurance is key. *"But don't just listen to God's word.* **You must do what it says. Otherwise, you are only fooling yourselves.** *For if you listen to the word and don't obey, it is like glancing at your face in a mirror. You see yourself, walk away, and forget what you look like."* {James 1:22-24 NLT}

*"***So prepare your minds for action** *and* **exercise self-control.** *Put all your hope in the gracious salvation that will come to you when Jesus Christ is revealed to the world.* **So you must live as God's obedient children.** *Don't slip back into your old ways of living to satisfy your own desires. You didn't know any better then. But now you must be holy in everything you do, just as God who chose you is holy."* {1 Pet 1:13-15 NLT}

"Dear friends, I warn you as "temporary residents and foreigners" to keep away from worldly desires that wage war against your very souls." {1 Pet 2:11} I love that verse! We are not at home here so don't get too comfortable. We are just passing through on our way to our final and eternal destination. Paul is begging us not to be lured off the narrow path. *"But our citizenship is in heaven, and from it we await a Savior, the Lord Jesus Christ,"* {Phil 3:20}

When we become a child of God, our citizenship has been instantly transferred. We have been relocated from this world to Heaven. We are indeed foreigners in this land. If you find that you are feeling uncomfortable in places or around people that you once enjoyed, this may be a good indication that you are heading in the right direction.

"If they have escaped the corruption of the world by knowing our Lord and Savior Jesus Christ and are again entangled in it and are overcome, they are worse off at the end than they were at the beginning. It would have been better for them not to have known the way of righteousness, than to have known it and then to turn their backs on the sacred command that was passed on to them. Of them the proverbs are true: "A dog returns to its vomit,"and, "A sow that is washed returns to her wallowing in the mud." {2 Pet 2: 20-22 NIV}

I believe it's fair to say that only believers fit this description. Peter isn't questioning the faith of his audience. On the contrary, he acknowledges it. What he does question, however, is the progress of their sanctification.

*"But, beloved, **do not forget this one thing, that with the Lord one day is as a thousand years, and a thousand years as one day.** The Lord is not slack concerning His promise, as some count slackness, but **is <u>longsuffering toward us</u>, not willing that any should perish but <u>that all should come to repentance</u>.** But the day of the Lord will come as a thief in the night, in which the heavens will pass away with a great noise, and the elements will melt with fervent heat; both the earth and the works that are in it will be burned up. Therefore, since all these things will be dissolved, **what manner of persons ought you to be in holy conduct and godliness, looking for and <u>hastening the coming</u> of the day of God,** because of which the heavens will be dissolved, being on fire, and the elements will melt with fervent heat? Nevertheless we, according to His promise, look for new heavens and a new earth in which righteousness dwells. Therefore, beloved, looking forward to these things, be diligent to be found by Him in peace, without spot and blameless; and consider that **the longsuffering of our Lord <u>is salvation</u>**—as also our beloved brother*

214

Paul, according to the wisdom given to him, has written to you, as also in all his epistles, speaking in them of these things, in which are some things hard to understand, which **untaught and unstable people twist to their own destruction, as they do also the rest of the Scriptures.** *You therefore, beloved, since you know this beforehand,* **<u>beware lest you also fall from your own steadfastness,</u> being led away with the error of the wicked;** *But grow in the grace and knowledge of our Lord and Savior Jesus Christ. To him be glory both now and forever! Amen"* {2 Peter 3:8-18}

We are advised that some of the Scriptures are hard for us to understand. But, we are also urged to beware of who we listen to for discernment and Godly counsel. Everyone has an opinion, however, according to Peter, there will be people who are both untaught and unstable that will try to teach us in error. Clearly, we should not blindly trust what people tell us about God's Word, regardless of whether they be parents, friends, preachers or teachers with seminary degrees. We need to test all of it against the authenticating light, the Bible. Another important nuance in this Scripture is that the Lord is described as "longsuffering. According to Strong's Concordance, the word "longsuffering" is from the Greek word "makrothumia," which means waiting sufficient time before expressing anger. This avoids the premature use of force [retribution] that rises out of improper anger [a personal reaction].

Did you notice that the verse we just read has suggested that we can hasten the coming of the Lord? Could we actually accelerate the Day by being a truly repentant people? The Lord is patient with us, in spite of our troubles and rebellion. He is longsuffering because He does not want us to perish in our ignorance, but He desires that we repent and grow in grace and in our knowledge of the truth. Don't' miss this! Peter says that the Lord's longsuffering "is" our salvation. These

215

passages suggest that as we pursue the process of sanctification, the Father's longsuffering and patience with us "is" salvation. He is compassionately giving us time to come to our senses. We have a good and loving father who *"is gracious and compassionate, slow to anger and rich in love."* {Psalm 145:8 NIV}

Why is it written that we should be "diligent" to be found "without spot and blameless?" Is this even possible? Doesn't God's grace cover all sin...the past, present, and future? Yes, I do believe that's true. So, what do you or I have to do with this process, and what is it that we should be diligently doing? In humility, we should be a repentant people with hearts that quickly turn from disobedience. His Lordship must govern our lives. *"But now is the time to get rid of anger, rage, malicious behavior, slander, and dirty language. Don't lie to each other, for you have stripped off your old sinful nature and all its wicked deeds. Put on your new nature, and be renewed as you learn to know your Creator and become like him."* {Col 3:8-10 NIV}

Once saved always saved? Think deeply about what the Scriptures are saying. I am sure that Jesus was not struggling to properly articulate Himself. He said what He meant and meant what He said.

"Now all has been heard; **here is the conclusion of the matter: Fear God and keep his commandments,** *for this is the duty of all mankind."* {Ecc 12:13 NIV} The gospel of grace leading to salvation with no call for righteousness has gone on for a long time, with little challenge. I believe that it has largely permeated the Church of our day.

I am urging you to give serious consideration to what you've read in this book. Don't blindly follow the masses. Even and especially if our culture encourages us otherwise, we must cling to the Word of God as our only source for absolute truth. Remember that Jesus said the way is difficult that leads to life and there are only a few that find it.

- Yes, we are justified by faith {Rom 5:1}, but our faith can cease to exist {Luke 8:13; Rom 11:19-23}

- Yes, we are not under the law {Rom 6:14,15}, but if you live according to the sinful nature you will die. {Rom 8:13}

- Yes, we are not saved by works {Eph 2:8,9}, but to receive eternal life and not destruction, we must sow to please the spirit and not the sinful nature. {Gal 6:8-9}

- Yes, God is faithful to us {1 John 1:9; 1 Cor 10:13}, but we must be faithful to Him and "remain in Him" until our last breath. {Rev 2:10-11}

- Yes, we have freedom in Christ {Gal 5:1}, but this freedom is not to willfully and blatantly disregard His will and indulge in our own sinful desires. {Gal 5:13; 1 Pet 2:16}

In the Epistles of Timothy, the Apostle Paul gives Timothy instructions. He tells him to pass these things on to other Christians and also to hold on to them for his own well-being and perseverance.

- *"Watch your life and doctrine closely. Persevere in them, because if you do, you will save both yourself and your hearers."* {1 Tim 4:16 NIV}

- *"Timothy, guard what has been entrusted to your care. Turn away from godless chatter and the opposing ideas of what is falsely called knowledge, which some have professed **and in so doing have departed from the faith.**"* {1 Tim 6:20-21 NIV}

- *"For certain individuals whose condemnation was written about long ago have secretly slipped in among you. They are ungodly people, who pervert the grace of our God into a license for immorality and deny Jesus Christ our only Sovereign and Lord."* {Jude 4 NIV}

The message Jude delivered was about teachers who will distort the grace of God into something very different – a license for immorality. The word 'deny' in the Greek can mean to disregard.

*"To the Jews **who had believed him**, Jesus said, "**If you hold to my teaching**, you are really my disciples."* {John 8:31 NIV}

The grace of God teaches us to live holy lives, *"For **the grace of God** has appeared that offers salvation to all people. It **teaches us to say "No" to ungodliness and worldly passions**, and to live self-controlled, upright and godly lives in this present age, while we wait for the blessed hope—the appearing of the glory of our great God and Savior, Jesus Christ, who gave himself for us to redeem us from all wickedness and to purify for himself a people that are his very own, eager to do what is good."* {Titus 2:11-14 NIV}

Paul's plea for us was to seek the true faith, and not fall prey to the teachings of counterfeit grace. This was not just a message for the early Christians. It is for all generations. Paul was adamant that, as Christians, we were entrusted with the gospel and that we must contend for it and stay faithful to its teachings, even in the face of persecution or death.

The True Gospel According to Paul:

*"Now, brothers and sisters, I want to remind you of the gospel I preached to you, which you received and on which you have taken your stand. **By this gospel, you are saved if you hold firmly to the word I preached to you. Otherwise, you have believed in vain.** For what I received I passed on to you as of first importance: that Christ died for our sins according to the Scriptures, that he was buried, that he was raised on the third day according to the Scriptures,"* {1 Cor 15:1-3 NIV}

Paul was saying we are saved by grace through faith in Christ, period. He strongly conveyed that this was a matter of primary importance, but this was not all that Paul preached and it was not the end of the story. *"Once you were alienated from God and were enemies in your minds because of your evil behavior. But now he has reconciled you by Christ's physical body through death to present you holy in his sight, without blemish and free from accusation— **if you continue in your faith, established and firm, and do not move from the hope held out in the gospel.** This is the gospel that you heard and that has been proclaimed to every creature under heaven, and of which I, Paul, have become a servant."* {Col 1:21-23 NIV}

"For I am not ashamed of the gospel, because it is the power of God that brings salvation to everyone who believes: first to the Jew, then to the Gentile. For in the gospel the righteousness of God is revealed—a righteousness that is by faith from first to last, just as it is written: The righteous will live by faith." {Rom 1:16-17 NIV}

- *"By this gospel you are saved, if you hold firmly to the word I preached to you. Otherwise, you have believed in vain."* {1 Cor 15:2 NIV}

- *"You can be sure that no immoral, impure, or greedy person will inherit the Kingdom of Christ and of God. For a greedy person is an idolater, worshiping the things of this world. **Don't be fooled by those who try to excuse these sins, for the anger of God will fall on all who disobey him.** Don't participate in the things these people do."* {Eph 5:5-7 NLT}

- *"Whoever sows to please their flesh, from the flesh will reap destruction; whoever sows to please the Spirit, from the Spirit **will reap eternal life.** Let us not become weary in doing good, for at the proper time we **will reap a harvest if we do not give up.**"* {Gal 6:8-9}

*"...so that, having been justified by his grace, **we might** become heirs having the **hope** of eternal life."* {Titus 3:7}

Why did Paul say that after we have been justified by His grace that we "might" become heirs? Paul said something similar in Hebrews 10:36. Some other translations say, "we should" others, "we may" and some "we might." What a curious choice of words!

*"Timothy, my son, I am giving you this command in keeping with the prophecies once made about you, so that by recalling them you may fight the battle well, **holding on to faith and a good conscience**, which **some have rejected and so have suffered shipwreck with regard to the faith.**"* {1 Tim 1:19}

We can be confident that His Word is complete truth, and His promises are indeed an assurance that He is always willing to hear our confessions, forgive our transgressions and help us through difficult seasons and situations. He will never leave us. *"So let us come boldly to the throne of our gracious God. There we will receive his mercy, and we will find grace to help us when we need it most."* {Heb 4:16 NLT}

"But if we confess our sins to him, he is faithful and just to forgive us our sins and to cleanse us from all wickedness." {1 John 1:9 NLT}

The warnings in the Bible highlight the fact that *sin* is our effort to feel secure in something other than God. He wants us to understand that the world is a trap for us. The warnings are for our own good. His ultimate desire is to bless and protect us if we will seek our security in His love, power, and promises. Regardless of what someone professes with their lips, if one claims to be a Christian but lives contrary to God's Word in a lifestyle of disobedience, then by their actions they have walked away from Jesus. ***"Such people claim they know God, but they deny him by the way they live.*** *They are detestable and disobedient, worthless for doing anything good."* {Titus 1:16 NLT}

It is only God Himself who knows if His Spirit was ever actually present in a person. But, one thing is certain, there will be many who thought they had salvation, and because of their miscalculation, they will be faced with the most devastating consequences one can fathom.

Let's review the truths we have established from God's Word. The Bible teaches us that salvation is a free gift. Grace is unmerited favor that we cannot earn and do not deserve. The only way to access our heavenly Father is through His Son Jesus Christ. It is through Christ alone that we are saved by grace. When justification occurs, we receive the indwelling of the Holy Spirit, which is a deposit within us on our future inheritance. It is by and through the Holy Spirit that we are enabled and empowered to overcome our desire to sin, so we can turn from it and adjust our lives as we remain in fellowship with Christ. It is our daily choice to remain or "abide" in Him. Thus, the apostles have sternly warned us to remain steadfast to the end, to overcome and to endure. We are told in the Bible that those who live according to the Spirit and not according to the flesh are under no condemnation.

However, if we choose to pursue our own plans for this life and if we reject or forsake our relationship with Christ, we do not have access to this promise, and we will reap what we sow. Jesus told us that if we sow to the flesh we will reap death. If it turns out that our reservation in heaven is canceled, the deposit returned, and the name blotted out, it will only be because of our rejection of truth. The fact is that we are called to obedience, and we have been given help from heaven to sustain us. It is a choice. Choose this day whom you will serve.

The enlightened realization that salvation can be lost might cause anxiety or fear, especially for those who have been taught and have believed otherwise. Take this to the Lord in prayer. He says that because He cares for us, we should cast all of our cares and anxieties on Him. When you take it to Him, He will speak to you and give you assurance and peace, but if needed, He may also bring conviction. Listen. Don't harden your heart or hide behind walls of pride or human wisdom. Scripture says that the Holy Spirit will bear witness that we belong to Him; He will also confirm the truth within our spirit. And don't be disheartened, there are just as many words of assurance in the Bible as there are words of warning.

As a child of God, we are not left alone. God is faithful. Our role is to elevate Him as the supreme King over our lives and to stay in the relationship with Him. Who is on the throne of your life, right now? Who or what is most important to you? If the answer is anyone or anything other than the Lord, a major adjustment is required.

The Lord is a jealous God. His jealousy is not like ours, it is a righteous and Godly jealousy. It does not come from a place of insecurity, pride, anxiety or frustration as ours would. He is jealous to defend the sovereignty of His Holy Name. He is jealous for us like a husband would be for the love and affection of his wife. God is love, but God is also truth. When we allow people to feel comfortable in their sin, it isn't helpful or loving towards them. God is calling on His true disciples to rise up with courage, emboldened by the power of His Spirit to share the truth of the Word, without fearing the opinions or reactions of men.

"Therefore, go and make disciples of all the nations, baptizing them in the name of the Father and the Son and the Holy Spirit. Teach these new disciples to obey all the commands I have given you. And be sure of this: I am with you always, even to the end of the age." {Matt 28:19-20 NLT}

The Bible will offend. It's not your Word; it's the Word of God. If you had a friend that was going to die, but you had something you could give her that would save her life, would you withhold it from her? In a world of opinions and a culture of deception, people desperately need the truth. *"For the word of God is alive and powerful. It is sharper than the sharpest two-edged*

223

sword, cutting between soul and spirit, between joint and marrow. It exposes our innermost thoughts and desires." {Heb 4:12 NLT}

For those that have spiritual eyes to see and ears to hear, let us stand by the path and share the truth of the full gospel to warn those entering the broad way. The Lord has promised that if we are faithful to share His Word, it will not return void. I pray that the Holy Spirit will go before us and prepare the hearts of those who hear this message to receive discernment and confirmation in the truth of God's Word. He is working in the hearts of His people to prepare His Bride. Jesus gave us His Word and His promises. He also prophetically told us what will happen in the "last days." He did this, so we could understand, discern and be spiritually awake when the time "of the end" was near. He said that those who belong to Him will not be caught by surprise. He also said that no man will know the day or the hour of His return, but He gave us detailed descriptions so the generations living in the last days would not be unaware.

"Now, brothers and sisters, about times and dates we do not need to write to you, for you know very well that the day of the Lord will come like a thief in the night. While people are saying, "Peace and safety," destruction will come on them suddenly, as labor pains on a pregnant woman, and they will not escape. **But you, brothers and sisters, are not in darkness so that this day should surprise you like a thief.** *You are all children of the light and children of the day.* **We do not belong to the night or to the darkness. So then, let us not be like others, who are asleep, but let us be awake and sober."** {1 Thess 5:1-6 NIV}

While it is true that when Jesus returns, the vast majority of the world will be without God, the Bible also says that many people will understand, prepare, and be ready. We all know that we are not promised tomorrow. If you stood before the throne of Christ next week, are you ready?

"Many will be purified, made spotless and refined, but the wicked will continue to be wicked. **None of the wicked will understand, but those who are wise will understand.** *"* {Daniel 12:10 NIV}

"And this world is fading away, along with everything that people crave. **But anyone who does what pleases God will live forever.** *"* {1 John 2:17 NLT}

CHAPTER THIRTEEN

S.I.P

How can we be certain we are "Remaining in Christ?" First things first, the foundation is the cornerstone. Our faith must be established on these three unchangeable biblical essentials [the gospel]:

1) Jesus is Lord, and He calls on us to submit to His Lordship.

2) Jesus died for us so that our sins can be forgiven.

3) Jesus has risen for us so that we can have eternal life.

Once our faith is rooted on this firm foundation, all of our relationships will be guided by the Holy Spirit. Bad habits and non-Christ like attitudes that were once immune to change, will become engaged in the process of transformation. We will no longer be comfortable with sin. The Holy Spirit will illuminate wrongdoing and He will help us become sensitive to it and make us aware of it. We will have new thoughts, new values, and new priorities. Many people become followers of Christ believing they can gain all of the benefits, like eternal security, without taking on any of the responsibility.

"Then He said to them, "Follow Me, and I will make you fishers of men." {Matt 4:19}

Right off the bat, Jesus was speaking directly to His new believers. He was letting them know that if they chose to be on His team, there is a lot of work to do for the Kingdom. It is a lifetime mission. *"We are therefore Christ's ambassadors, as though God were making his appeal through us..."* {2 Cor 5:20 NIV}

We know that Jesus values family relationships. The Bible is full of exhortations to husbands, wives, and children which encourage us to be like Christ in all we do. But Jesus also said this: *"Do not think that I came to bring peace on earth. I did not come to bring peace but a sword. For I have come to 'set a man against his father, a daughter against her mother, and a daughter-in-law against her mother-in-law'; and 'a man's enemies will be those of his own household.' He who loves father or mother more than Me is not worthy of Me. And he who loves son or daughter more than Me is not worthy of Me."* {Matt 10:34-37}

Whoa. What? This sounds so outrageous and contradictory to Jesus' teachings. But, it's not at all. The point Jesus was making is that our relationship with Him should come before any other relationship that we have. If we are genuinely committed to Christ, it may cause problems with family members or friends who may not understand why we are dropping bad habits or bad influences. They may not be on board with our resolve to remain faithful to a new course for our lives.

*"When He had called the people to Himself, with His disciples also, He said to them, **"Whoever desires to come after Me, let him deny himself, and take up his cross, and follow Me.** For whoever desires to save his life will lose it,*

but whoever loses his life for My sake and the gospel's will save it. **For what will it profit a man if he gains the whole world, and loses his own soul? Or what will a man give in exchange for his soul?"** {Mark 8:34-37}

Be prepared to give up the world and the things of it. Jesus said that it won't matter if we have attained all the wealth and power the world can offer us, it's a bad trade. Don't take the deal. Nothing is worth trading your soul. How many followers of Christ give up their souls for much less than all the world can offer? Some people walk away from Christ because they just refuse to let go of relationships with certain people. Others turn back to the world because they're too busy with their own plans and ambitions. Don't get caught in the trap of pursuing the cares and pleasures of life. Good intentions will not amount to anything, so don't trust yourself with how you "feel" about spending time with God... just do it. Make an appointment with Him in your day timer if that works best for you. Make it happen. It's the most important meeting of your day.

Many people want to do the right thing, and they have good intentions, but they keep putting it off until "tomorrow." They think they have plenty of time and that eventually they'll do it...just not now. You know what, for many people, tomorrow never comes. The enemy uses distractions to keep us away from the things that will help us grow in our relationship with God. He may keep us so busy with the chaos of life, our jobs and raising a family, that we never even notice that we've put everything else in front of our time with the Lord. If we truly love God and are sincere and committed to follow Jesus, we will understand that this commitment includes making time for Him and then doing whatever He asks of us. He will ask us to do what is necessary, and if He has revealed something to us that needs to be adjusted, He expects us to do it right then.

We need to mature in Christ.

"Then we will no longer be infants, tossed back and forth by the waves, and blown here and there by every wind of teaching [false doctrines] and by the cunning and craftiness of people in their deceitful scheming." {Eph 4:14 NIV}

False doctrine is not simply about worshipping another god. You can believe in Jesus as the Son of God and still be taught and believe a false doctrine about Him and about salvation. This verse is plainly exhorting believers to pursue Christian maturity by studying the pure Word of God. When we study the Word of God for ourselves, we will be able to discern the difference between what is true or false when we hear it. There is a lesson in the Apostle Paul's encouragement of Timothy. Paul cared for Timothy like a son in the faith. He made a significant personal investment, training him in the spiritual things. Let's consider his advice. Paul warns Timothy:

*"Timothy, **guard what has been entrusted to your care.** Turn away from godless chatter and the opposing ideas of what is falsely called knowledge, which some have professed and in so doing have departed from the faith."* {1 Tim 6:20-21- NIV}

Paul was spurring Timothy on to maturity in the things of Christ. We must be aware of the danger of taking the things of God for granted and the perils of trying to do everything on our own, without depending on the power of the Holy Spirit.

We need to stand firmly rooted in God's grace.

"You, then, my son, be strong in the grace that is in Christ Jesus." {2 Tim 2:1 NIV} The things we "do" after our faith has been established through Christ, is merely a response to His lavish grace and the overwhelming love of God. It is only through the power of His grace that we can stand firm in Him with all the authority of Heaven. Christianity is not just a religious belief, it is a personal relationship with Jesus that leads to a transformed life! It is an entire lifetime of joyful submission to the Lord. Through our obedience, we are covered by repentance, confession, forgiveness and peace.

"We can give without loving, but we cannot love without giving." This quote has been attributed to many people, so I'm not certain of the original author, but I am quite certain that it is a true statement. There are three areas of giving that we should continually consider:

1) **Our Time.** Time is our greatest commodity. We should seek to invest our time enriching the lives of others, bringing glory to the Lord and blessing His people. The enemy knows that tempting us with evil would be too obvious, so he will lure us away with distractions, leaving us with no time for God. Be sure to invest your time wisely.

It will likely not be evil endeavors that will steal our time. There are plenty of "good things" that can suck away all of our time. We need to consider whether or not we are sacrificing what is best for what is good. I'm sure you realize that there will always be "good things" we can be doing. We need to ask the Lord what He wants us doing. We should be intentional about pursuing "God things" instead of "good things." Time is our greatest gift and our most valuable commodity. We can never get it back.

2) **Our Talents.** We should use our God given abilities to serve others and to help build up the Church.

3) **Our Treasure.** We are stewards of all that God has entrusted to us. We are expected to be a blessing with the resources we've been given.

A few years ago, I was reading verses in the Bible about tithing. Admittedly, I almost fell out of my chair when I found a promise from the Lord. God even said, "Test me on this." So, here is the promise: if we are faithful to tithe as the Lord has commanded us, He has promised to bless us. But this is not why I got excited. The next verse says this, (drumroll please) "I will rebuke the devourer for your sakes..." Okay, now I am listening! This is a spiritual principle and promise that comes with an exciting key to victory. God has promised to rebuke Satan's attacks against us if we are faithful to do what He has asked by tithing. This is a compelling promise, and I can testify that the Lord is faithful and true to His Word. I still get attacked by the enemy, but I'm not worried because the Lord is true to his promise and He is my shield and my defender. It is as if the attacks fall to the ground with no effect.

*"Bring all the tithes into the storehouse, That there may be food in My house, And try Me now in this," Says the Lord of hosts, "If I will not open for you the windows of heaven and pour out for you such blessing that there will not be room enough to receive it. **And I will rebuke the devourer for your sakes,...**"* {Mal 3:10-11}

As children of God, talking with Him is one of the most powerful benefits we have. But, our prayers are not designed for us to inform God of our needs. He has assured us that He already knows what we need, even before we call on Him. {Isa 65:24}

Well, then, what is the purpose of our prayers? Through prayer we experience God more intimately. When a child experiences the loving provisions of a parent, they become more confident and convinced of the parent's unrelenting love for them.

- *"Be anxious for nothing, but in everything by prayer and supplication, with thanksgiving, let your requests be made known to God;"* {Phil 4:6}

- *"Therefore humble yourselves under the mighty hand of God, that He may exalt you in due time, casting all your care upon Him, for He cares for you."* {1 Pet 5:6-7}

- *"...The effective, fervent prayer of a righteous man avails much."* {James 5:16}

Our prayers are effective when we pray the Word of God, because the Word of God is the will of God. As a follower of Christ, we have put on His righteousness by grace through faith. In Christ, we've been given authority and dominion over every force of the enemy. Our prayers will be powerful and effective for bringing down strongholds, but the power is activated by our faith. We need to believe God is able and that He will do what He has promised in His Word.

"For the weapons of our warfare are not carnal but mighty in God for pulling down strongholds, casting down arguments and every high thing that exalts itself against the knowledge of God, bringing every thought into captivity to the obedience of Christ." {2 Cor 10:4-5}

God wants to show Himself strong on our behalf. He involves us in the process through prayer, so we are in an active relationship with Him. Without the two-way communication of prayer, we might just chalk the Lord's favor and provisions up to coincidence. The Holy Spirit actively brings the Word of God to our hearts. He speaks to us in many different ways, but the place where God has promised to speak is in the Bible. I just can't say it enough...we need to read God's Word, trust His Word and obey His Word. We should strive to be a people that are committed to live under God's authority.

*"You, however, must teach what is appropriate to sound doctrine. Teach the older men to be temperate, worthy of respect, self-controlled, and sound in faith, in love and in endurance. Likewise, teach the older women to be reverent in the way they live, **not to be slanderers or addicted to much wine**, but to teach what is good. Then they can urge the younger women to love their husbands and children, to be self-controlled and pure, to be busy at home, to be kind, and to be subject to their husbands, so that no one will malign the word of God. Similarly, encourage the young men to be self-controlled. In everything set them an example by doing what is good. In your teaching show integrity, seriousness and soundness of speech that cannot be condemned, so that those who oppose you may be ashamed because they have nothing bad to say about us... For the grace of God has appeared that offers salvation to all people. **It teaches us to say "No" to ungodliness and worldly passions, and to live self-controlled, upright and godly lives in this present age, while we wait for the blessed hope**—the appearing of the glory of our great God and Savior, Jesus Christ, who gave himself for us to redeem us from all wickedness and to purify for himself a people that are his very own, eager to do what is good. **These, then, are the things you should teach**. Encourage and*

rebuke with all authority. Do not let anyone despise you. {Titus 2:1-8, 11-15 NIV}

Jesus encouraged His followers as He said, *"For my yoke is easy, and my burden is light."* {Matt 11:30 NIV} That may sound a little baffling considering that He also said, *"If you love Me, keep My commandments."* {John 14:15 NIV}

It may seem complex but, it really isn't difficult. We don't need to focus on His commands. We need to focus on Him. It's as simple as that. If we are genuinely committed to spending time with Him, we will experience transformation by the renewing of our mind and our heart. Our strength will come from the Lord.

We are strengthened in two ways:

1) through time in the Word of God, and

2) through worshipping Him.

When asked, what is the most important or the greatest commandment? *Jesus replied: "'Love the Lord your God with all your heart and with all your soul and with all your mind.'* **This is the first and greatest commandment."** {Matt 22:37-38 NIV}

He wants our heart and our sincere devotion. He wants our devoted love, and in return, He says we cannot even comprehend what he has in store for those that love Him... *"No eye has seen, no ear has heard, and no mind has imagined what God has prepared for those who love him."* {1 Cor 2:9}

I can't even imagine missing out on this. I am standing in agreement with all of my brothers and sisters in Christ.

"Please Lord, prepare us to know you in a more meaningful way. I pray that you will draw us into your Word and strengthen us by your Holy Spirit, confirm your truths in our hearts and minds. Increase our faith and help us to know and understand the depths of your love. Help us to be faithful stewards, to serve You and build Your Kingdom. Provide us with all that we need to fulfill Your plans and purposes. Protect us from the plans the enemy has for us and let them fall to the ground with no effect. I pray for an increase of spiritual strength and wisdom to flow within the body of Christ. Convict our hearts in the areas that need to be purified, cleanse us from pride and our self-serving motives and cause us to walk humbly before you. Let us not be wise in our own eyes or opinions. We pray for our pastors and the leaders that are guiding your people. Help us to be spiritually alive, alert and awake. Bring us to a place of genuine repentance and restore us for your glory. Yours is the Kingdom and the power and the glory forever and ever. In the mighty name of Jesus Christ, Amen!"

My friend Chris Grant shared a powerful spiritual concept with me. He said, "We need to sip Jesus all day." Of course, I had to ask him to elaborate on that. He replied, "S.I.P... think of it like taking a cup of coffee with you throughout your entire day. You need a little sip of Jesus when your boss is overbearing. You will probably need a sip of Jesus when your kids are using magic markers on the wall. You need a sip of Jesus when you're tired, frustrated or overwhelmed." He said, let me explain what a sip looks like, it is...

Sacrificial. Intentional. Purposeful.
"Sometimes, we need to be intentional with our time. We should be attentive and alert, so we will be aware and recognize when the Lord has someone in

our life that needs our help or guidance. We need to take time to listen, time to share, and time to care about someone else in the same way that the Lord cares for us. When we are committed to our Savior and we allow Him to alter our plans, the joy of the Lord will be our strength." {Neh 8:10}

Well, it's time to wrap this up, so let's be on guard because the world will continually entice us to compromise the truth; however, when we were born again, God deposited the Spirit of truth into us. This is awesome because the role of the Holy Spirit is to guide us in all truth. *"...when he, the Spirit of truth, comes, he will guide you into all the truth."* {John 16:13 NIV}

Jesus warned and comforted the disciples, *"But these **things I have told you, that when the time comes, you may remember that I told you of them**... In the world you will have tribulation; but be of good cheer, I have overcome the world."* {John 16:4,33} *"I am God, and there is no other; I am God, and there is none like me, **I make known the end from the beginning, from ancient times, what is still to come**. I say: **My purpose will stand**... **what I have said**, that I will bring about; what I have planned, **that will I do."** {Isa 46:10-11 NIV}

"...Save yourselves from this corrupt generation." {Acts 2:40} Don't trust the world for spiritual guidance, remain in Christ and rely on His Word as the filter for genuine truth. Earnestly study the Scriptures for yourself, "rightly dividing the Word" as if your life depends on it...because it does.

Don't die in the pew.

NOTES

Chapter 1

Requiem for the Shekel
HAARETZ Feb 24, 2012
https://www.haaretz.com/1.5190129

[Priscilla Shirer Quote]
https://churchleaders.com/daily-buzz/269988-priscilla-shirer-can-you-tell-the-difference-between-right-and-almost-right.html

[Charles Spurgeon Quote] Apologetics 315 – Sun, Feb 3, 2013
https://apologetics315.com/2013/02/charles-spurgeon-on-discernment/

Chapter 2

[Three Categories of People that are addressed in the Bible]
Dr. Billye Brim – How to Rightly Divide the Word (Part 1): p. 13, 14 Branson, MO: A Glorious Church Fellowship, Inc. Published 2016

[Israel History]
https://www.jewishvirtuallibrary.org/the-two-kingdoms-of-israel

https://www.jewishvirtuallibrary.org/the-babylonian-exile

[Mark Twain Quote]
https://quoteinvestigator.com/2016/12/03/misinformed/

Israel Medical and Technological Advances
[Artificial Cornea, Robotic Exoskeleton]

https://www.israel21c.org/the-top-12-most-amazing-israeli-medical-advances/

The Jerusalem Post – Aug 1, 2017

[Drip Irrigation Technology] https://www.jpost.com/Business-and-Innovation/6-incredible-Israeli-discoveries-that-influenced-the-world-501332

[Instant Messaging] https://reformjuda-ism.org/blog/2018/02/27/7-decades-innovation-israel-comput-ers-and-software-technologies

[Iron Dome, USB Flash Drives, Pill-Cam, Voice Over IP, GPS Smartphone app] https://en.wikipedia.org/wiki/List_of_Is-raeli_inventions_and_discoveries

[Israel Nobel Prize Winners since 1966] https://en.wikipedia.org/wiki/List_of_Israeli_Nobel_laureates

[How Israel Became The Startup Nation Having The 3rd Most Companies On The Nasdaq] Seeking Alpha by Steven M.Wil-liams - Feb 27, 2018 https://seekingalpha.com/article/4151094-israel-became-startup-nation-3rd-companies-nasdaq

The Jerusalem Post – [Revival of the Hebrew Language] By Daniel Bensadoun Oct 15, 2010 10:37 https://www.jpost.com/Jewish-World/Jewish-News/This-week-in-history-Revival-of-the-Hebrew-language

Chapter 3

[Definition of Death in Greek] Strong's Concordance https://biblehub.com/greek/2288.htm

[Definition of Remain in Greek] Strong's Concordance https://biblehub.com/greek/3306.htm

Chapter 5

[Definition of Strive in Greek] Strong's Concordance https://biblehub.com/greek/75.htm

[Definition of Disqualified in Greek] Strong's Concordance https://biblehub.com/greek/96.htm

[Definition of Seared in Greek] Strong's Concordance

https://biblehub.com/greek/2743.htm

Chapter 6

[Early Church Doctrine]
https://www.neverthirsty.org/bible-qa/qa-archives/question/did-the-primitive-church-preach-the-doctrine-of-once-saved-always-saved/

[Early Christian Period] https://www.jewishvirtuallibrary.org/pharisees-sadducees-and-essenes

[Zealots] https://www.jewishvirtuallibrary.org/the-great-revolt-66-70-ce

[History of Christianity - Reformation]
http://www.newworldencyclopedia.org/entry/History_of_Christianity

[Dates of the Epistles]
https://www.blueletterbible.org/study/pnt/pnt02.cfm

[New Testament not circulating until the 4ᵗ Century]
http://www.historyworld.net/wrldhis/PlainTextHistories.asp?historyid=aa11

https://www.christianitytoday.com/history/issues/issue-43/how-we-got-our-bible-christian-history-timeline.html

[John Chrysostom]
https://en.wikipedia.org/wiki/Adversus_Judaeos

Parkes, James. Prelude to Dialogue (London: 1969) P.153; cited in Wilken, p. xv.
["the most horrible and violent denunciations of Judaism to be found in the writings of any Christian theologian."]

Flannery, Edward H. The Anguish of the Jews, New York, N.Y.: Macmillan Publishing Cp., Inc. 1965, p.49,48
["lustful, rapacious, greedy, perfidious bandits, inveterate murderers, men possessed by the devil."]

Hagee, John Why Christians Should Support Israel, San Antonio, TX: CUFI University Press. 2016

[Crusades - p.39-40] [Spain – p. 45-46] [Martin Luther – p. 40-41]

Gritsch, Eric W. (2012). Martin Luther's Anti-Semitisim: Against His Better Judgment. Grand Rapids, Michigan: William B. Eerdmans Publishing Company. ISBN 978-0-8028-6676-9. Pp. 86-87 ["the devil's people." "envenomed worms" expelled "for all time."]

Brecht, Martin, Martin Luther, tr. James L. Schaaf, Philadelphia: Fortress Press, 1985-93, 3:214
["There was a world of difference between his [Luther's] belief in salvation and his racial ideology. Nevertheless, his misguided agitation had the evil result that Luther fatefully became one of the 'church fathers' of anti-Semitism and thus provided material for the universal hatred of the Jews, cloaking it with the authority of the reformer."]

Todd, Obbie Deep South Reformation, Am I Saved? A Brief History of Assurance: Aug 22, 2016
https://deepsouthreformation.com/2016/08/

[Great Awakening]
https://www.history.com/topics/great-awakening

[Protestant Church Beginnings – Timeline]
http://protestantism.co.uk/denominations

Chapter 7

[Definition of Disqualified in Greek] Strong's Concordance
https://biblehub.com/greek/3404.htm

Irenaeus Against Heresies Public Domain Originally Published 1885: 1.26.3; 3.10.6

http://www.earlychristianwritings.com/text/clement-stromata-book3-english.html

RENNER Who were the Nicolaitans, and what was their doctrine and deeds? Aug 27, 2016
https://renner.org/who-were-nicolaitans-what-was-doctrine-deeds/

Chapter 9

[Definition of Hypocrite in Greek] Strong's Concordance
https://biblehub.com/greek/5273.htm

Chapter 11

[Definition of Longsuffering in Greek] Strong's Concordance and
Helps Word Studies
https://biblehub.com/greek/3115.htm

NOTES:

NOTES:

NOTES:

NOTES:

The Lord is waking up His Bride.

www.dontdieinthepew.com

If this booked has been a blessing to you then share it with a friend or your pastor.

Krista Smith is the President of a Christian Academy in Greenville, SC, and the founder and former CEO of mortgage lending firm Solverus Banc. She served as the Executive Director for Heartstep Foundation from 2004-2016.  She has been an avid student of the Bible since her childhood and has been involved in ministry and leading Bible studies throughout her adult years. Krista has been a serial entrepreneur for over twenty years, until the Lord asked her, "Who's kingdom are you building?" Her journey of faith includes over three decades of biblical study, a prophetic dream in 2005 and an urgent message for the Church.